SURVIVE & THRIVE POST-PANDEMIC

A GUIDEBOOK FOR LEGAL & PROFESSIONAL SERVICES PROVIDERS

JULIE SAVARINO, MBA, JD

Published by Business Development Inc.
Print ISBN: 978-1-7329453-3-3
Ebook ISBN: 978-1-7329453-4-0

DISCLAIMER: This book and its contents are provided on an "as is" basis and no representations or warranties of any kind are made. Content contained or made available through this book is not intended to and does not constitute specific advice for any individual firm or professional. The publisher and the author do not make any guarantee or other promise as to any results that may be obtained from using the contents of this book. As this is a business, professional, and legal-services book, out of an abundance of caution, no direct information or references are made to specific health or virus-related issues.

20% of the net proceeds from this book will be donated to Global Giving, a highly rated charity which is the largest global crowdfunding community connecting nonprofits, donors, and companies in nearly every country.

www.GlobalGiving.org

WHAT READERS SAY ABOUT *SURVIVE & THRIVE*

"This book contains a bounty of valuable strategies, ideas, tips and techniques to help professionals build and recover in the wake of the pandemic."

—Chris Poole, President and Chief Executive Officer, JAMS

"This is a very well done and useful book. All lawyers and other professionals need a guidebook like this to help them navigate post-pandemic."

—Gina F. Rubel, Esq., Founder & CEO, Furia Rubel
Communications, Inc.

"This book is timely, comprehensive, practical, immediately actionable, and invaluable."

—Ralph Baxter, Former Chairman and CEO, Orrick
Legendary Leader Inspiring Global Change in Law

"This book is *the* go-to, client-centric resource for all professional services providers and firms."

—Cammie R. Teems, CP, Risk Manager, Bestway USA

"This is a must-read written by a master in client development and relations. Any lawyer or other professional interested in getting the best results from the time they invest in building their practice should read and use this book."

—Stephen Crossman, Vice President & Head of Sales Chief Growth
Officer, SurePoint Technologies

"This book is packed with practical and proven strategies and tactics firms and practitioners can put to immediate use."
— Liam Brown, Founder, Chairman and CEO, Elevate Services

"This book contains a wealth of invaluable and pragmatic information."
— Roy Sexton, Director of Marketing, Clark Hill PLC

"Any professional who wants to take their professional services practice to the next level should read this book."
— Jillion Weisberg, Account Director, Kira Systems

"This book in comprehensive, practical, and immediately actionable."
— Mary Jennings, Director of Human Resources, Sandberg, Phoenix & von Gontard

"This is an extremely timely book that contains and abundance of great content."
— Kim Easterle Mattes, Producer, Aon Risk Solutions

"If you are not sure what to do to build your practice and firm after a pandemic, this book is for you."
— Stephen McGarry, Founder of Lex Mundi, World Services Group, LawyersAccountants.com, AILFN, HG.org, and RFP

"*Survive & Thrive* contains great information, strategies, and tips. This will be a valuable reference point to help grow our practices as we emerge from the pandemic."
— Andrew Barnes, Chief Executive Officer, Harwood Andrews and Sladen Legal

CONTENTS

HOW TO GET THE MOST FROM READING THIS BOOK

In order to get measurable results that drive your survival and future growth and development, your key takeaways from this book must be made actionable.

Each professional practice and firm* is a bit different, consisting of numerous variables, such as type of practice, target markets, strengths, preferences, skills, knowledge, and many other variants, so the most relevant takeaways from this book must first be identified and then tailored for each firm to put to use to get results.

The forgetting curve states, if there is no attempt to retain information gained, within about twenty-four hours, people will forget at least fifty percent of what they take in.[1] Don't let the time you spend reading this book be wasted!

I suggest formally capturing the content most relevant to you as you read this book, because simply reading it, setting it aside, and eventually forgetting about it will not necessarily help you survive and thrive after a pandemic.

Once you purchase this book, consider:

* Setting aside time to read it.

* While reading it, take notes in writing of the content that resonates most with you, preferably using an automated word-processing program. (Doing so will make it easiest and

least time-consuming for you to actually use the information you gained from reading this book.)

* Dogear or place a sticky note on relevant pages.

* Highlight text or otherwise mark or save the content, ideas, strategies, tips or techniques you think are best to help you or your firm survive and thrive.

Capturing in writing that content you believe will be most useful to you or your firm simultaneous to your reading (or shortly after reading) this book is the best use of your limited available time. Remember: getting measurable results from what you gained from this book is a process that takes focus and effort over time.

*All professional service providers and firms, whether solo, small, or large, are *firms,* and will often be referred to simply as *firms* throughout the book.*

INTRODUCTION

Pandemics bring the world to a standstill. All economies are based on confidence, yet during and after a pandemic, uncertainty and fear abounds.

The entire professional services sector the world over—which includes law firms, accounting firms, brokerages, consulting firms, etc.— are cash-based, people-centric, and relationship-driven businesses. The rapid changes to relationships—both professional and personal—caused by a pandemic are structural and deep.

The definition of "business as usual" is altered, and all professional services providers need to adapt and change quickly to respond to the new ways that employees, clients, and everyone else will behave, communicate, buy, and use their services in the future. The speed at which information travels will not slow down.

This guide book will help you regain a sense of control and certainty by allowing you to determine the next best steps to build your practice or firm in the wake of the 2020 crisis.

To sustain profitable growth amidst post-pandemic uncertainty, lawyers, accountants, brokers, consultants, in-house business professionals, and any other professional services providers and firms need actionable information. The good news is there are things that have been done and can be done to minimize the negative consequences of a pandemic, both at the firm and individual practitioner levels. This book contains a plethora of immediately usable and actionable information, including:

> ➤ Proven strategies, tactics, tools, and techniques

> ➢ What worked, what did not during the 2020 crisis
> ➢ Real-life success stories and examples
> ➢ Tips and suggestions from clients of professional services firms
> ➢ Wisdom from some of the world's leading experts (all are listed in Appendix 4)
> ➢ Key takeaways and checklists, and many other resources

Who is this book for?

Both professional services firms *and* individual professional services providers, including those who are fee-earners and those business professionals who support fee earners.

Whether you are a solo practitioner or work in a small firm, a boutique, a large firm, or another type of professional services firm, this guidebook is for you, because it will lead you through what you can do to develop and grow your practice in order to survive and thrive after a pandemic or other economic crisis.

Professional services as defined in this book

Professional services are occupations in the economy requiring special training, skills, or knowledge. Some professional services require holding professional licenses, such as accountants, attorneys, architects, brokers, and engineers.

Other professional services involve providing specialized business support to professional services firms and other businesses, including consulting, business development, human resources, marketing, SaaS, sales, technology, business management and operational advice, counsel, solutions, and services.

*All of these service providers, whether solo, small, large, partnerships, LLCs or other operating entities, are *firms*, and will often be referred to simply as *firms* throughout the book.*

The content in this book has been sourced from the author's knowledge and her over thirty years' experience working for and with hundreds of law, accounting, architecture, financial services, SaaS, and consulting firms. It is drawn from working with the owners, partners, practitioners, vendors, and business professionals employed by those firms, as well. Additional sources for the following information are cited in the endnotes and in Appendix 4, which includes those interviewed and quoted. Other resources and references used to write this book can be found here:

https://busdevinc.com/select_bibliography.html.

1

LESSONS FROM THE 2020 GLOBAL ECONOMIC CRISIS

> Once the fog lifts from the coronavirus crisis, every professional needs to dust themself off and work to understand and embrace the inevitable changes in the way business will be conducted from now on.
>
> – Ralph Baxter [2]

Crises are opportunities to make (or break) your reputation.

Reputations are built and spread based on what people say and communicate to others. Both in good times and in bad, every professional needs to balance the immediate with the long-term, in order to be known and remembered for the "right" reasons. What are the right reasons? Usually they are a combination of the firm or practitioner's mission, vision, and values. Or, it's the answer to the question, "What do we/the firm/you want to be known and remembered for?"

Almost all professional services firms and providers seek to nurture and develop strong, productive relationships with their entire ecosystem, both internally and externally, and both personally and professionally, as appropriate.

At all times, decisions, actions, and communications should consider the best interests of the firm, its clients, and all stakeholders. An empathetic and added-value tone will always increase the strength of stakeholder relationships. This is even more important to employ in a post-pandemic environment, when fear and uncertainty will continue on many levels.

In a crisis, the need for sensitive and understanding communications rises to a new level. Yet, such traits do not come easy for many lawyers and other highly educated professional services providers (See Chapter 4, *Personal Style*). Ignoring the emotional and psychological needs and preferences of the people with whom you interact at this critical stage can, in fact, produce adverse effects. (The importance of "people" to all professional services firms is discussed in detail in Chapter 3 of this book).

The lesson here is simple: Do not use a pandemic or other crisis as an opportunity to sell or push your services. In times of crisis, it's best to be a resource to clients and contacts. In all communications, strive to be understanding, helpful, and/or useful. Nothing illustrates this need better than the complaints of clients heard all across social media during the 2020 crisis, where "selling" services was perceived as opportunism in the face of tragedy. Many took offense. Others passively agreed.

What works?

❖ Embrace a new relationship reality. Learn to interact, meaningfully, without being physically present.

❖ Personalize all your verbal and visual communications.

Colin S. Levy currently serves as corporate counsel at Salary.com, where he leads all legal operations, processes, and procedures for the company. He works with numerous legal and professional services firms and their professionals to provide guidance and support. He is a leading voice on legal technology and legal innovation issues, and he is a sophisticated buyer and user of outside professional services.

Over the past ten years, Levy has selected, hired, and worked with dozens of law firms and other professional services firms. He says, "Being human is at the heart of every successful client relationship, especially during challenging times. New business results from sincere, authentic relationships based on caring, trusting, and proactively reaching out to clients, and letting them know you are there for them. Don't try to sell. Instead, initiate a sincere and natural conversation with your client. Doing so will be well-received by your client and allows you to develop and build your personal and professional relationship."

For over thirteen years, Jeff Carr served as general counsel for FMC Technologies, (www.FMC-technologies.com), where he has vetted, hired, and worked with many lawyers, law firms, and other professional services providers. He is widely considered a pioneering innovator in the way law firms, lawyers, and clients do business. He says, "Especially during crises, clients don't want content. They need actionable answers and solutions, because they need to act." In good times and bad, no client ever wants to be sold, they want their problems solved, period.

Here is a LinkedIn post I did on this topic, "6 Best Practices in Client Communications, Content Creation & Delivery in the New Normal" (complete with hashtags):[3]

6 Best Practices in Client Relations, Content Creation & Delivery in the New Normal

Presented By: Julie Savarino

From a webinar hosted by SurePoint Technologies, available to view on demand here - http://info.sppc.com/webinars

1. Consider the client's perspective. Don't just add more generic crisis-related content by sending summaries of the provisions of a new law or regulation. Analyze and translate it into a useful information and a user-friendly format.

2. Clients do not want content. They need and want actionable answers.

3. No one has the luxury of time right now. Clients want easily digestible information in a useful format that can be used or shared quickly. Think checklists, FAQs, charts, and online tools like Chicago accounting firm Grant Thornton's excellent Risk Assessment, at www.grantthornton.com/COVID-19-resource-center/pandemic-rapid-response-assessment.aspx. Think about organizing all crisis-related resources and content by business problem/issue/question, industry or type of entity, or by role, e.g., board members, human resources, etc.

4. Consider asking all your important clients, referral sources, and others in your ecosystem these three key questions:

    a. How are you (and yours)?

    b. Is there anything you or your company/organization need?

    c. How can I help?

5. Capture all commonly asked questions in one place, then analyze and use them to create and share future content that is compelling, useful, informative, helpful, and timely.

6. Strategically leverage spoken content. Convert it to writing, because most people are visual learners, i.e., they prefer to gain new information by reading or seeing it. For example, leverage the content from recent webinars/podcasts by reviewing the slide deck or notes; select a few of the top takeaways; and share those with clients in an email or post on LinkedIn.

During any crisis, time is of the essence. In early to mid-March 2020, clients eagerly read the first few emails they received about the crisis. But once dozens a day or more started arriving—one or more from every single firm they have ever communicated with—the number of emails became overwhelming. The reading stopped. Firms that delivered the same or very similar information in non-user friendly or non-useful manners did not stand out. It is always critical to make your business communications better and/or different, if you want to be well thought of or remembered for the right reasons.

Be a giver, be generous

A great example of what works was posted on LinkedIn, titled "Radical Generosity,"[4] authored by Robert Glazer, Founder and CEO of Acceleration Partners.

> In the face of the 2020 crisis, rather than retrench and become paralyzed, Justin Essner, a regional sales manager Hilton Hotels in Orlando, decided to invest and empathize. He listed his top 36 relationships and sent each of them a customized gift: A high-end bottle of tequila in a plastic box that read "Break in Case of Emergency," surrounded by caution tape. Justin also included a handwritten note telling his event planner clients that he knew times were tough, but that he and his team were thinking of them. Within days, he received dozens of thank you texts from grateful event planners, the same people who had been calling days earlier to cancel events worth millions of dollars. Some of the event planners were also looking forward. Justin received two requests for future events in 2021, one for $500,000 and the other for $1.2 million. While these types of potential bookings won't make up for his losses, they are helping steady the ship.

Deliver information that clients want and need, in the format they want and prefer (not just during a crisis)

Content fatigue is a real thing any day of the week, but even more so when it comes in a deluge of emails and webinar offers on similar, non-distinguishable topics and issues during and after a pandemic. And when communications are not sent in a format that your clients prefer, they end up in the trash. Numerous posts on LinkedIn and Twitter confirm this.

Take my LinkedIn post, for example, which highlighted in-house counsel feedback on content fatigue. The post got over 5,000 views and sixty comments in less than three days and was trending in hashtag #Lawyers.

So, what do GCs and in-house counsel want, don't want, and need from lawyers and law firms right now?[5]

1. Send fewer mass emails and webinar offers regarding the 2020 crisis. If you must, personalize the message to include relevant and specific information on how it could impact the client's business. Offer brief analysis; something truly helpful.

2. Be a trusted advisor. Do some homework. Instead of sending a mass email, your client may prefer a personal, private phone call. There, you can direct the conversation according to their specific business interests—on a non-billable basis.

3. Before calling:

   a. Research and monitor the client's business. Take note of potential risks, warning signs, and legal issues that might be specific to the business. Know in advance how your firm could help in specific situations.

   b. Scan the horizon. Summarize in bullet-point format the latest developments as they apply to the client's business, including what to expect, what's developing, and future issues of which to be aware. Clearly communicate what you are ready and able to support.

   c. Think and create. Take time to consider new, better, or value-added ways to support and assist clients though this challenging time.

4. Provide direct, straightforward advice and guidance. Clients want issues summarized, followed by practical legal advice and guidance they can use for their companies, or share with their leadership.

5. Assign and suggest talented, diverse professionals (not just practicing lawyers) who can offer possible solutions and options.

6. Suggest and offer innovative technology options. Support #legaltech and #legalops.[6]

Avoid making the mistake of assuming the benefits and features that you value in your services are the same as what existing and potential clients desire. Yes, clients hire professionals for their skills, but they also want to know how that knowledge will save them time and money or bring them value.

Other common mistakes

At all times, but especially during crises, time is a limited, valuable, and a too-scarce commodity for every business professional. Firms and practitioners need to send information in the format clients prefer (not in legalese or lengthy documents) and that acknowledges those limitations.

People consume new information in two main ways: either by seeing it (reading articles, books, and documents, or watching television, videos, devices, etc.) or by hearing and listening to it (in phone calls or discussions audiobooks, podcasts, etc.). Various studies suggest most people are visual learners, i.e., many prefer to consume new information seeing or reading it rather than by listening to it.

Yet, most highly educated professionals tend to prefer using their sense hearing above others. They are auditory learners, i.e., they gain most of their information from what they *hear* or *listen to*, setting up an unconscious bias toward delivering most information verbally. So, it follows that many make the mistake of not converting spoken content into written form to reach both visual and auditory learners.

For example, remarks made during live presentations, webinars, and podcasts can readily be repurposed into writing and used for blogs, alerts, and social media, which will appeal to visual learners. Firms that do not practice converting spoken words into writing and repurposing the content miss a significant part of the market.

In addition, too few firms and providers carefully consider or view their mass emails from the client's perspective before sending these types of emails. Because I am a client of—or referral source to—many law and professional services firms, I receive a lot of them, from all over the world.

From my perspective, and from that of other law firm clients and referral sources, firms and practitioners need to reevaluate and reconsider their:

Email subject lines

As of April 4, 2020, I have received over 300 emails from professional services firms with the subject line containing "FIRM NAME – CRISIS NAME UPDATE #___" (to date, I have received #s 1 to #20 or more from many firms) or "FIRM NAME – 'CRISIS NAME' - Volume ___," plus many others with subject lines similar to the above but without the firm name. Numbering and volume numbers have no relevance to clients, nor are they much use to them.

The numbering of external emails does not allow clients to read, organize, or use the content in any efficient, useful manner. Nor is it relevant to use the terms "e-Update" or "eAlert" in your email subject lines—everyone knows it is an e-communication! The use of these types of subject lines seems to be a holdover from the early days of emailing, and the numbering system is likely an archaic, firm-centered way to internally track and send mass emails. Firms should consider removing the use of "e" references, numbers, and/or volume numbers in the subject lines of *any* emails to clients. Instead, use the space to include the issue or problem(s) the email addresses.

Some examples of compelling subject lines from the 2020 crisis include: Business Continuity Considerations; CARES Act: Business Tax Summary; Summary of Families First Act; "Crisis" Employment Law Checklist; SBA Loan Eligibility; FAQs Paycheck Protection Program Loans SBA/Treasury; and Telemedicine in the 2020 Pandemic: What Has Changed and What Has Not.

Before and during the 2020 crisis, the best emails offered valuable yet complimentary services or practical, immediately usable tools or solutions, some even offered automated apps.

Email content must pack value, be relevant, or it will be ignored.

The objectives of all client communications—email, phone, online—during and after the pandemic are two-fold. They must balance a sincere desire to understand client needs against your need to sell and stay relevant (and prosperous) in a changing market, e.g., secure new matters and clients. For some, this will be very challenging. Yet, with forethought, any firm or practitioner can do this.

Many firms' mass client emails are sent from an email address that already has the firm name in it, such as:

FIRMNAME@Domain_name.com.

Having the firm name in both the "from" email address and subject line is redundant, unnecessary, and takes up valuable real estate at the top of the email, which is needed to make a strong first impression and capture readers' interest.

In the future, consider sending a test email to a few individuals, asking them to review it from a client's perspective and offer edits/changes. Make those before sending.

Here are some more tips:

Mass emails should succinctly digest helpful information and suggest ways you/your firm can assist in finding a solution right now or in the future. Especially consider how the content of the email will or does impact the client. Ask yourself:

- ✓ What's the impact of the information contained in this email to the client's business/from the client's perspective?

- ✓ What is the exact value the information in this email delivers to the client/audience?

- ✓ Can the reader quickly discern the substance of this email from the subject line?

- ✓ Is the firm name already contained as part of the sender's email address? If so, does it need to appear in the subject line also?

- ✓ Is the content of this email written in executive summary form?

- ✓ What is of most use or interest to the reader in this email?

- ✓ From the client's perspective, is the information contained in this email helpful, useful, and/or valuable to the client/reader? If so, how so?, etc.

Which SBA Loan Option is Right for My Business?

Loan Name	Economic Injury Disaster Loan	Paycheck Protection Program
Who lends the money?	You interact directly with the SBA	You interact directly with your primary banking institution
Where do I apply?	www.sba.gov or via mail in application	Directly with your bank once SBA makes the application available
Who is eligible	Businesses with < 500 employees	Businesses with < 500 employees with certain exceptions
What does the loan cover?	Operating expenses over the next 6 months	Payroll expenses from Feb 15, 2020 - June 30th, 2020
What is the maximum loan amount?	$2,000,000	$10,000,000
Does it require personal guaranties?	Yes	No
Does it require collateral	Yes for loan > $25,000	No
What is the initial repayment terms	No payments through the first 12 months	No payments up to first 12 months
What are the repayment terms after initial period?	30-year term loan	10-year term loan
What is the interest rate during the term out period?	3.75% for for-profits, 2.75% for non-profits	4%
Is the loan forgivable	No	Yes
Does the loan have a prepayment penalty	No	No
What is the estimated time from application to receiving loan funds?	3 - 4 weeks	1 - 2 weeks
Are there any fees?	Minimal recording fee	No
Is this loan part of the CARES Stimulus Package?	No	Yes
How much is allocated nationally towards this loan program?	$50 billion	$350 billion
Who should apply?	Businesses that don't have an immediate need for a cash infusion but anticipate needing a source of low cost funding to handle operating expenses during the downturn and additional support to help the business coming out of the downturn	Businesses that need an immediate cash infusion to help keep employees on the payroll and businesses that may need additional support paying mortgages, rent and utilities through June 30, 2020

Subject to final regulations forthcoming from the United States Small Business Administration

BOK Financial® is a trademark of BOKF, NA. Member FDIC. Equal Housing Lender. © 2020 BOKF, NA.

The image above is one example of a very effective email sent by BOK Financial, www.bokfinancial.com, during the 2020 crisis. All of the company's small business clients received it within less than 36 hours after the CARES Act was signed into law in the United States. The considerable effort, focus, time, and energy invested in preparing this chart was time well spent, because the end result was extremely timely, useful, and helpful to many of the bank's customers.

Leverage the content from webinars and podcasts

A plethora of webinars and podcasts were offered and promoted in response to COVID-19, yet few summarized, emailed, or posted any highlights or key takeaways to LinkedIn or other social media after they ended. This is a missed opportunity.

Posting interesting, informative, helpful, and useful content such as checklists or key takeaways after webinars/podcasts are over can and will increase your online reach, reputation, potential new leads, and followers.

How to remedy?

1. Appoint a scribe or experienced content writer/producer to take notes during the webinar/podcast.

2. After it ends, have them summarize the key takeaways, best practices, useful PowerPoint slide(s), or other valuable or useful content covered.

3. Draft and have an experienced person review it before posting to LinkedIn, Twitter and other relevant social media.

4. Post it with the best, most relevant hashtags.

LinkedIn Posts: Mistakes and Opportunities

Related to the above, most firms post the exact same or very similar content contained in their emails or blog posts on LinkedIn. This is a major mistake and missed opportunity during and after a pandemic when physically in person, face-to-face meetings are not possible.

Why is LinkedIn so important, especially during social distancing? Because LinkedIn has the largest (or one of the largest) global B2B reach of *any* media, whether traditional or online. LinkedIn has over 260 million active users, and over 575 million user profiles, the vast majority are business professionals.[7] Currently on LinkedIn, there are over eleven million profiles with the title of CEO or equivalent and over 1 million with general and in-house counsel titles. No other single media comes close to that reach. Yet, most firms and practitioners have vastly underutilized the power and reach of LinkedIn—before, during, and after the 2020 crisis.

Few firms have a strategically organized approach or program to make the best use of LinkedIn to optimize the use of the firm's company page, individual practitioner profiles, posts, messaging, or the other tools and features on LinkedIn.

For example, few firms create and post compelling LinkedIn posts. Rather, they favor post firm-centric information about firm events, webinars, alerts, speaking roles, or other firm news. From the client's perspective, while that may be marginally helpful, what's really in it for them? Rarely do we see posts that summarize key takeaways from the presentations they give, useful things to consider or articles they write, nor do most posts include calls to action.

What is a call to action (CTA)?

Again, firms and practitioners miss a significant opportunity by not posting compelling, useful, and client-centric content on LinkedIn.

During the 2020 crisis, several firms posted all or most of their client alerts onto LinkedIn as PDF files. This is another mistake. Lengthy PDF documents are not easy to read on LinkedIn, and downloading them requires precious time that readers do not necessarily have. Few professional services firms have institutionalized the capability to download alerts and white papers from social media with one click.

In addition, few firms or practitioners know how to write optimal LinkedIn posts and use the most appropriate hashtags effectively.

A great example of a timely, helpful and useful post on LinkedIn was done by the 160-lawyer firm, Kelley Kronenberg. They quickly created an innovative crisis-focused Text Hotline and posted it on LinkedIn:

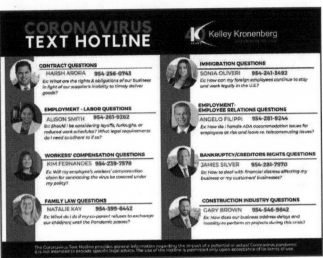

Also, on LinkedIn, most firm's company pages have relatively very few "followers." Many of the world's leading accounting and consulting firms have *millions* of followers on their LinkedIn company pages, while most other professional services firms have less than .5-1% of that number of followers.

Whether for the firm itself or for individual providers, now is the time to create and implement a strategic plan to optimize the use of LinkedIn, upgrade posts, use of messaging, and increase your number of followers.

Offer new, innovative corporate citizenship or added value solutions, offers, services, and resources

Resource Centers

As of mid-April 2020, unless your firm was first-to-market (see the story about KL Gates below) or very early to launch a crisis-focused Resource Center, if you still want to join in, *avoid naming it "Resource Center."* Why? Because, by the time this book is published, almost every major law firm and other professional services firm has some variation of a "Resource Center" (RC). There are thousands now, and most are indistinguishable from one another.

RCs are designed to compile all the firm's content, alerts, thought leadership, insights, and other relevant information in one place to make it easier for the firm's clients and visitors to access the firm's crisis-related knowledge. In theory, it is a smart move. In practice, you need to take some time to think it through. (Even existing RCs might benefit from some self-examination and changes.)

In addition to your RCs' name, make sure to organize the information so users can easily find what they are looking for. Content should be categorized or organized by topic/problem/issue from the client's perspective. Many of the early RCs are organized by publication date, with the most recent files displaying first. This is a lost opportunity to maintain relevance after the initial blow of the crisis.

While publication date does add context, things change quickly, and some information becomes less important as time goes by. But older content may remain relevant. Proper navigation tools and content organization will help users, long after the initial period, find what they need quickly. One RC that defines its target market focus as part of its RC is Paul Weiss's, which says, in part, "Providing guidance for boards and management..." The target market is defined from the client's perspective in the tag line descriptor.

As Jeff Carr says, "Clients don't want content, they need actionable answers. For example, can I take the temperature of my employees before they enter the office?"

Now is the time to review your firm's existing RC, and consider what updates, changes, or enhancements would make it more valuable to clients. If you're just pulling one together, make sure to implement these suggestions.

An example of being first to market, to gain first-mover advantages

What are the benefits of being first to market on anything new, developing, or latent? First movers gain a competitive advantage because they usually establish and strengthen brand recognition, client loyalty, get new opportunities and new business, and gain time to develop, enhance, and scale their offerings ahead of competitors.

K&L Gates recently gained first-mover advantages because it was one of the first firms to go to market offering a value-added service to address legal needs resulting from the 2020 outbreak—its resource center.

On March 9, 2020 (at least two weeks before the majority of law firms and other professional services firms posted anything about the 2020 crisis), K&L Gates announced a global, multi-disciplinary crisis task force, along with a complimentary online resource center with sample employment policies, fact sheets, checklists, and more. They invited clients, viewers, and readers to visit the firm's groundbreaking, client-focused, and award-winning digital content site, K&L Gates HUB, and the new 2020 crisis resource section. The firm frequently updates the HUB with timely information, insights, upcoming webinars, and other useful resources. (Find it at www.KLGatesHub.com)

Wondering how K&L Gates was able to coordinate and respond so quickly, I asked Craig Budner, Global Strategic Growth Partner at K&L Gates LLP, to share how the firm was able to coordinate, mobilize, and communicate so quickly and usefully about the developing 2020 crisis during such a challenging time.

He said, "K&L Gates does not simply talk about being globally integrated and collaborating in innovative ways. In fact, our firm's compensation system rewards it. As a result, innovative ideas and concepts are regularly shared internally, and viable ones are not ignored or dismissed by firm leaders as readily as they may be within other major law firms."

The firm has formal time codes for all lawyers' non-billable work and efforts, which are calculated into the firm's compensation process and decisions. So, K&L Gates lawyers who spend non-billable time on strategic and productive efforts, such as industry and practice-specific thought leadership and content generation, are rewarded for both their efforts and results. Budner says, "Just like in hockey, our firm keeps score by counting not just goals but also assists, by giving lawyers credit for non-billable work. So, we are not slowed down by internal arguments over who gets credit."

Another feature about K&L Gates that led to this successful effort is the firm is organized by and operating under a matrixed structure, which includes both formal practice area groups *and* industry groups. Budner attributes the maturity of the firm's organizational model as a reason that, as early as mid-February 2020, firm lawyers were quick to share with firm leaders the increasing number of questions their groups were receiving from clients about global health-related and economic issues.

Budner explains, "This gave us a head start to proactively think about the crisis from the clients' perspective."

As a result, the firm made three strategic and tactical decisions in late February and early March.

1. First, internally, they created a dedicated Task Force named C19TF, which included five partners and other key stakeholders.

2. C19TF then worked with others to set-up a new, dedicated, internal email group where every lawyer could send the questions they had received from clients and offer their expertise on any crisis-related issue, as well as other related information. This dedicated email group created a repository of information from the client's perspective. Budner says, "To borrow a phrase from hockey legend Wayne Gretzky, we were trying to see where the puck was heading."

3. The firm then created a dedicated crisis portal on their K&L Gates HUB, where many complimentary resources relating to the crisis were posted. They also offered secure, subscription-only access at a low flat fee to clients, which gave subscribers access to updated information on regulation changes.

Budner says, "Our new 2020 crisis HUB has received lots of great feedback, generated a lot of goodwill, and has also resulted in many new matters and engagements."

He and the K&L Gates team continue to analyze all new information and developments to create crisis-related content, offerings, and products that are relevant to and will be useful for their clients and others. But they also recognize that clients are overwhelmed with crisis-related emails and webinars. As a result, in addition to aggregating content, they are focusing on direct client engagement and virtual roundtables. Through these roundtables, clients can hear from their peers and subject-matter experts as to how best to respond to the issues as they arise.

Corporate Citizenship During a Pandemic

A great pro bono initiative that demonstrated proactive corporate responsibility and community stewardship was launched early on in the 2020 crisis in mid-March by the chairman of Paul Weiss, (www.paulweiss.com), Brad Karp. He announced a firm and region-wide pro bono effort to coordinate major law firms in the New York City region to help address legal needs resulting from the crisis, as reported by Kathryn Robino in *Above the Law*.[8]

Another innovative and generous effort in response to the 2020 crisis that stands out as better and different was rolled out in late March by Jack Newton, CEO and Founder of Clio (www.clio.com), and author of *The Client-Centered Law Firm*.

On behalf of Clio, Jack announced a $1 million fund to help those in need within the legal community. Jack says, "As part of our disaster relief program, Clio committed $1 million to help lawyers and law firms navigate the difficulties that lie ahead. While much of what lies ahead is uncharted territory, this remains clear: We need to undertake a swift and massive transformation of the legal industry, and compress change that would have transpired over the course of years into change that needs to happen over a course of weeks."

Hear from CEO and Co-founder Jack Newton

The funds will be used to support Clio licenses and implementations, provide financial aid for law firms and legal organizations, and support the education initiatives of bar and law societies around the globe. As this book goes to press, Clio has been inundated with applications, which the Clio team is currently in process of analyzing.

Many clients' wants and needs are still not currently being met (or are delivered and met, but in a less than satisfying way)

Even before the 2020 crisis hit, many professional services firms and providers were not a hundred-percent certain what their clients and other stakeholders want, need, or desire (in a statistically valid manner). Many firms and professionals *assume* or *presume* they already know what their clients need and want. They make broad and specific judgments or assumptions about clients' needs, wants, and preferences based mainly on what they have heard from some (but not a representative sample of) clients, from anecdotes heard from colleagues, or one-off feedback from clients.

Bill Bernbach, an advertising legend says, "It took millions of years for man's instincts to develop. It will take millions more for them to even vary. It is fashionable to talk about changing man. A communicator must be concerned with unchanging man, with his obsessive drive to survive, to be admired, to succeed, to love, to take care of his own."[9]

If you or your firm have not conducted a statistically meaningful client survey, now is the time. Carefully consider, "What can our firm/I do to provide better, faster and/or less expensive services?" Read on to learn what works.

Key Takeaways

This chapter is not necessarily exhaustive or complete. It is a summary and snapshot as of mid-April 2020. No doubt, there are and will be more lessons to be learned, along with other best practices and key takeaways from the 2020 crisis.

However, here are some key points at the time this book was written:

➢ Crises are opportunities to make or break your reputation, make sure to add to your reputation!
➢ Consider the client's perspective in everything you communicate. Be more client focused.
➢ Embrace a new, social distance relationship reality and master ways to interact without being in physical contact.
➢ Personalize and tailor all your communications.
➢ Be a giver, be generous.
➢ Deliver information that clients want and need, in the format they want and prefer (and do this *all the time*, not just during a crisis).
➢ Carefully review email subject lines before sending.
➢ Leverage the content from webinars and podcasts.
➢ Optimize your use of LinkedIn.

- ➢ Be different and better—create and offer new, innovative, corporate-citizenship-centric or added-value solutions, offers, services, and resources.
- ➢ Know clients' problems, pain points, wants, and needs, and strive to create cost-effective solutions to meet them.

2

WHAT WORKED FROM PAST ECONOMIC UPHEAVALS

> As history tells us, the firms and practitioners who adapt to the new realities the fastest and most strategically will likely be the ones who benefit the most in the future.
>
> – Gerry Riskin [10]

There are many useful and inspirational lessons to learn about how companies and firms have successfully weathered prior economic storms, then survived and thrived.

Both professional services firms and individual professional services providers can take lessons and get inspired by what has worked from the Great Depression, previous recessions, and other past economic downturns.

As the writer and philosopher George Santayana said in 1905, "Those who cannot remember the past are condemned to repeat it."

Nancy F. Koehn holds the James E. Robison Professor of Business Administration chair at Harvard Business School (HBS) and is the author of the highly rated book, *Forged in Crisis: The Power of Courageous Leadership in Turbulent Times,* which explains how five of history's greatest leaders managed crises and what can be learned from their experience.

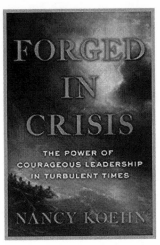

Professor Koehn was interviewed by *The Wall Street Journal* in 2009 on how companies survived earlier economic storms.[11] Below are key takeaways from this article (adapted and updated for the current crisis context):

1. **Being a natural and brilliant salesman** has helped many innovators and business owners weather depressions, recessions and other economic storms. For example, Henry Heinz, founder of Heinz Ketchup (now a Kraft brand). Henry figured out innovative ways to delay wages and get his employees to come back to work. He also renegotiated his rental contracts to reduce his rent to half price.

   Even if you are not a natural-born salesman (which many lawyers and other typically introverted professionals are not), now is the time to start thinking more like an entrepreneur.

   Entrepreneurship is defined this way by Howard Stevenson, professor at Harvard Business School and godfather of entrepreneurship studies: "the relentless pursuit of opportunity without regard to resources currently controlled."

Since many professional service providers are hired and paid to find ways to eliminate, reduce, control, or manage risk, becoming a full-fledged entrepreneurial thinker is not realistic. Instead, professionals can learn to consider and take more strategic risks. (Find suggestions and how-tos in Chapter 10.)

But first, ask yourself, "If I was just starting my practice, on my own and with limited resources, what exactly should I do to focus my business development in the most cost-efficient and effective ways?" (See options in Chapters 9 and 10.)

A related lesson is to make time to strategically think ahead, and be prepared for the unexpected. Remaining in a reactive, fear-driven panic mode often results in short-term decisions that may save money, resources, or time, but also may backfire or yield unintended consequences in the future. So, it's crucially important for all professionals to remain calm, think logically, and consider the best interests of the firm or practice in both the short and long term.

2.   **Don't cut back on marketing, just strategically realign it.** A major lesson from past economic downturns is the need to market, market, market, but to do so in strategically innovative and novel ways. For example, during the Great Depression, Proctor & Gamble (www.us.pg.com) decided to start marketing on the radio (which was like the Internet at that time). They created short audio dramas, which later helped coin the term "soap operas."

> To survive and thrive, all lawyers, firms, and other professionals must continue to invest in strategic marketing, selling, and related communications. Few firms or individual professionals without an effective marketing and sales program ever survive economic disruptions.
>
> – Ralph Baxter

3. **If possible, don't cut back on innovation, research and development (R&D).** Instead, strategically commit talent and resources to focus on how to do what you already do differently, better, faster, and/or less expensively.

    Few firms have a dedicated R&D or Innovation department, committee, executive, or any organized R&D or innovation effort of any kind. Instead, they rely on ideas generated every so often by members of the firm who happen to have the internal power and influence to get the R&D or innovation idea funded, planned, and implemented.

    Now is the time for all firms and practitioners to get more innovative in an organized, productive, and most potentially profitable manner. (Some strategic suggestions to do so are described in Chapters 6-9.)

4. **Do business and practice with people you trust,** treat them fairly, and when "it" hits the fan, they will be more loyal and less likely to back out.

    If there is one thing the COVD-19 pandemic should remind us, it's the importance of people. Without people, there is nothing to do, no law to practice, no accounting to be done, nothing. The next section of this book discusses the importance of people in more depth.

Lessons from the mid-1990s Recession

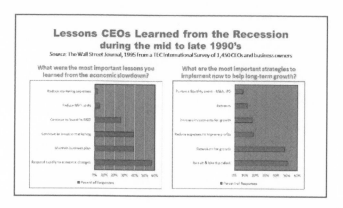

An article published in *The Wall Street Journal* in 1995 summarized the findings from a survey of business leaders conducted that year. The top-five lessons from CEOs on how to survive and thrive during an economic downturn and recession were:

1. Respond rapidly to economic changes

2. Recruit and hire top talent

3. Reposition company/firm for growth

4. Maintain business plan(s)

5. Continue to invest in marketing

Most law firms and other professional services firms are cash-based businesses, where cash is king and there are little (if any) retained earnings, so the instinct to save as much cash as possible during any economic downturn is a prudent strategy. But if taken too far, cutting costs to bare bones can make firms and practitioners vulnerable.

According to a study published by Bain in 2019[12], the companies that were among the eventual winners after a recession moved deliberately to capture opportunities before the recession. While they focused intensively on cost transformation, they also looked beyond cost. The winners excelled in four areas:

1. Early cost restructuring

2. Financial discipline

3. Aggressive commercial plays

4. Proactive mergers and acquisitions (M&A)

Companies can gain market share and profitability using the right strategy for the business cycle.[13]

Lessons from the 2008 Recession

From SunTrust Research[14], conducted in Q1-2019 of 516 businesses with annual revenue between $5 million and $250 million, during the 2008 recession, 86% of $50 million-plus public companies shrank. Yet, 14% continued to grow (at a 9% rate) by acting early, maintaining a long-term perspective and focusing on growth, not just cost cutting.

The 14% of public companies that grew:

1. Acted early

2. Took a long-term perspective

3. Focused on growth, not just cost cutting[15]

As reported in *Harvard Business Review*, companies that already made investments in digital technology, analytics, and agile business practices are usually better able to understand the economic threats of a downturn and respond more quickly.[16] Recessions can create wide and long-standing performance gaps between companies. Research has found that digital technology can do the same. Companies that have neglected digital transformation may find that the next economic downturn/recession makes those gaps insurmountable.

Other business practices and related disciplines are applicable to all professional services firms, yet not all firms or practitioners use or apply them. The remaining chapters in this book contain information on which business practices and disciplines are important to the survival and growth of professional services firms, how they apply to the professional services sector, and they describe specific ways to optimally deploy them.

Permanent economic changes from past downturns impacting the legal industry

A survey of large law firms conducted in 2013 found that firm leaders admitted the Great Recession-driven changes to clients' demands for more predictable, transparent, and reasonable pricing and increased efficiency were here to stay.[17]

Yet, firm leaders also acknowledged in 2013 that internal resistance slowed their response to adapting, upgrading, or changing their firm's strategies and tactics. Will the same hold true after the 2020 pandemic?

In an effort to reduce and control his company's total spend on outside legal services, Jeff Carr, who served as general counsel for FMC Technologies from 2001-2014, created the Alliance Counsel Engagement System (ACES), a method of hiring outside counsel that emphasizes value and goals[18]. ACES has been a model that many other legal industry entities, firms, alternative service providers, and SaaS solutions have borrowed from since.

In addition, the Association of Corporate Counsel's Value Challenge was created by then-general counsel of ACC, Susan Hackett, and was influenced by Jeff Carr's leadership.[19] Nowadays, most general counsel and other law firm clients continue to put mounting pressure on law firms to reduce the lack of predictability, transparency, and total outside legal services costs.

As a result of this increased pressure, many law firms created legal project and knowledge management departments, programs, and systems to become more efficient in the delivery of outside legal services. They have also been forced to respond to requests for proposal (RFPs) that now include online, reverse auctions, using automated platforms such as PERSUIT, BanyanRFP, RFP360, and others.

The need for all professional services firms and individual professional services providers to adjust, adapt, and make appropriate changes is a constant, yet especially so during and after pandemics or other economic crises.

Key Takeaways

- ➢ Embrace the new realities and changes ,and work to adapt to them.
- ➢ Consider what's worked in the past and how those lessons may apply to you and your firm.
- ➢ Take a long-term perspective and focus on strategic growth.
- ➢ Embrace a more business-like, entrepreneurial mindset and approach.
- ➢ Avoid the natural instinct to cut costs to the bone.
- ➢ Strategically realign your marketing and business development costs and efforts.
- ➢ Assess and upgrade your innovation and R&D.

3

YOUR MOST VALUABLE ASSET IS *PEOPLE*

If there is one thing we learned from the 2020 crisis, it's that *people* make the world go around. Without people working and interacting, the economy and our world as we know it comes to a standstill.

Embrace the new relationship reality

The success of all firms is driven by relationships with people and all people and relationships have been altered in many ways as a result of the pandemic. A pandemic causes rapid and deep structural changes to relationships, both professional and personal.

As human beings, when our health is threatened, our (relative) feelings of safety and security are shattered. The 2020 crisis brought disruption to every person on the planet to one degree or another, and the impacts will reverberate for some time. Without a feeling of (relative) safety, certainty, and confidence, no human being can function at an optimal level. For many people, these insecure and unsafe feelings may never completely go back to the "normal" of pre-crisis. For example, will physical office buildings and spaces be used as much and considered important in the future?

In order for a firm to survive and thrive post-pandemic, it is critically important for all professional services providers to understand and embrace the fact that each person, each client, and each referral source has and will continue to have varying levels of fear, unease, and acceptance. As a result, people will adapt their behavior and communications in different ways.

Emotional and physical impacts on people from the 2020 crisis

The emotional toll the 2020 pandemic has taken and will continue to take on all people, including professionals, is significant and should not be underestimated.

As a result of the 2020 crisis, we know for certain that all people, to one degree or another:

- Feel a lack of safety, control, freedom of movement, and the ability to chose
- Face abnormal levels of uncertainty and do not know what to expect
- Will continue to make efforts to stay six to fifteen feet away from other people when out

Most people are experiencing severe threats to their basic need for safety and security, and many are also experiencing threats to their fundamental need for shelter and food. Below is an image that illustrates Maslow's hierarchy of needs, a psychological theory that describes the pattern through which human motivations generally move. It postulates that for motivation to arise at the next stage, each stage must be satisfied within the individual themself.

Most people also experienced or continue to go through the five stages of grief as defined in the Kübler-Ross model, an image of which appears below.

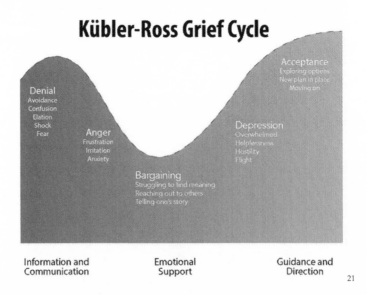

Embrace the fact that you are in the "people" and relationship business

All professional services firms and all professionals the world over are in the business of serving *people*. Without people, whether as individuals or in groups working in a company or entity, there is no professional service to deliver, because there would be no clients to serve, no law to practice, no deals to broker, and no advice to provide. Make no mistake: we are all in the people business. Lawyers and other professional services providers tend to think of clients as organizations or companies. It's important to remember that *people* hire you.

Because all professional services providers serve people, the most valuable asset in any professional services firm and for any professional services provider is *people*. This includes internal colleagues and external clients, experts, referral sources, suppliers and vendors, and even people you have not yet met or strangers you come across in the elevator, in coffee shops, or at sporting and other events, etc.

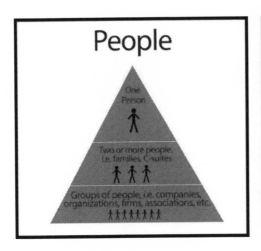

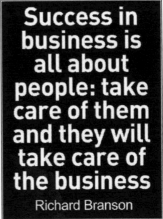

A major buyer of outside legal services, consulting, and accounting services recently said, "Clients, colleagues, and all people are the most valuable part of your practice. Any action, effort, and communication

47

made with sincere humanity, integrity, and a desire to help will build goodwill." So, being human-centered and meeting clients and customers where they are as human beings is more important today than ever before.

Relationships are everything in professional services practices because, without clients, we would have nothing to do. Yet, many professionals tend to:

- Define "client" as a corporation or organization, when all a corporation consists of are people. Only people can hire and retain professional services providers, whether on behalf of a company, organization, or for themselves or their family.

- Take many of their critical business relationships for granted.

- Think they already know everything about each of their clients.

- Remain mainly reactive, waiting for clients to call or reach out to them.

- Minimize the extent and degree to which change is constantly happening, both within both their clients' companies/entities and as to what is worrying individual clients.

Due to non-stop competitive pressures and the innovative things some firms are doing to get new clients, all professional services providers need to be more vigilant in protecting their relationships, and in nurturing, securing, adding value to, and developing them regularly, as appropriate.

How you interact with other people, both at work and outside work, is the foundation to a successful professional practice, whether you are a lawyer, architect, doctor, or other type of business professional. Everything you do, say, and communicate (no matter if it's in person or electronically) immediately reflects upon you and either increases or diminishes your reputation, the word-of-mouth others say about you, and/or the quality of your relationship with any person you interact with, both personally and professionally.

What you do, say, or write and how you do it, how you behave, and how you conduct yourself are critical. This is especially true before being retained or getting new work. You are evaluated/judged by all people you meet and know, and by existing clients, prospective clients, referral sources, and each stranger at all times. No professional is *entitled* to be called or contacted by their clients or anyone else. It must be earned.

An issue facing many highly educated professionals is they are not natural "people" persons. Instead, studies show, the more educated a person is, the more introverted they tend to be, meaning most of their attention is paid to what's inside their heads, not what is happening around them.

Yet, many "natural" rainmakers tend to be "people" persons. Many self-made businesspeople also tend to be natural "people" persons. As Richard Branson, the extraordinarily successful and serial entrepreneur who founded the Virgin Group, says, "I love people. Love spending time with people. I love learning from people."

Branson is a bit of an outlier, as a natural people person. Many of the rest of us who are professional services provider need be aware and take steps to balance the potentially negative behaviors our natural introversion causes in order to recognize and maximize our relationships with people.

Know where business originates

Even without in-person physical contact, very little professional services work (for a person, family, or company/organization) is awarded and won without some level of interpersonal communications with one or more clients, prospects, and/or referral sources. Preferably, this occurs through a physically in-person meeting, but if that is not possible, it can be via a secure videoconference. Either way, routinely getting face-to-face with clients and at every appropriate opportunity remains the most effective business and client development tool for all professionals.

Every human being has the potential to be a referral source, to some degree—to be someone who provides free word-of-mouth advertising about you and/or your firm that can add to or detract from your reputation. So, making it your standard approach to lead with a pleasant, kind, respectful demeanor toward every person you meet or run across tends to pay off. One never knows from whom the next piece of work or referral may come!

Many highly educated professionals proceed through life regularly communicating with and running into many people, through meetings, work, schools, events, conferences, activities, boards, etc. Yet most fail to keep track or formally capture many of these people in any organized or useful manner.

Relationships with people are nebulous, so maintaining them in an organized manner over the course of a career takes more than memory. It takes discipline. Some best practices to be sure you capture all (or most) people you meet, work with, or know include: asking for business cards/beaming v-cards and setting up a system (either with or without assistance) to add them to your automated contact system, and then sending each new acquaintance a connect request on LinkedIn. LinkedIn makes it very easy to keep track of people when they change positions or move (but you first must be connected to them on LinkedIn).

Maintaining an automated Rolodex or list of every person you know or have met is critical to having the most successful career possible, because all professional practices revolve around people!

It's also important to learn, know, absorb, and use the current *science* about people. The study of human behavior, psychology, personal styles, and interpersonal communications has uncovered many statistics and generalities about human behavior. Even without referring to any specific science, common sense tells us that every person:

* Is born with or has evolved into having certain natural behavioral tendencies, communication styles, thinking patterns, personal preferences, and other idiosyncrasies unique to him/her.

* Thinks and works differently and has their own way of learning and taking in new information.

* Has strengths and weaknesses in their own personality and personal style. No one has a "perfect" personality or style; we are all human with faults and attributes.

* Very few people think, act, or view the world/reality in the same way. Variations and differences are by far the norm, i.e., approximately 70% to 80% of the people you meet over your lifetime will think and behave differently than you do.

* Has their own personal motives, values and agenda and their own business motives, values, and agenda.

Science has demonstrated that all people:

* Acquire and process information using three stimuli: visual, auditory, and kinesthetic (based on feeling).[23]

* Most people are primarily visual and then auditory learners, but all people also use feelings to some degree.

* A large percentage of the world's population are *visual* learners. This means they remember things better when they look at them, see them, or read them over the use of any other sense.

* The most predominant sense preferred by most highly educated professionals to acquire and process information is hearing/auditory, i.e., professionals tend rely more and default to talking or hearing.

* Express a certain amount of emotion through their voice and body when they communicate. As a rule, owners, leaders, entrepreneurs, and CEOs tend to be strongly emotional communicators.

* Express a certain amount of assertiveness when communicating. As a rule, owners, leaders, entrepreneurs, and CEOs also tend to be strongly assertive communicators.

Relentlessly commit to diversity

Diversity is a term that refers to people of various backgrounds, races, religions, genders, orientations, etc. Because people are the most valuable and most significant driver to the success of any firm or profession, it is important to view people holistically, as one. Just because someone is a different gender or race does not make them less than any other human being. Yet, due to explicit and implicit or unconscious bias that all human beings have, it is not always easy to treat all people with equal courtesy and respect.

Many professional services firms are majority owned and operated by one type of person, whether mostly white males, white females, African Americans, or those who identify as LGBTQ+. Having only one set of people thinking and considering any subject or topic and then making decisions will narrow the perspective and inputs considerably.

Studies show that adding diverse voices, thoughts, ideas, and opinions can yield greater results. According to research, increasing diversity results in better decision-making because diverse groups/teams outperform individual decision makers sixty-six percent of the time. Decision-making improves as team diversity increases.[24]

For example, a few years ago I was with an African American friend of mine in New York City. We were downtown on three different occasions and needed to catch a cab. Each time, she volunteered to hail a cab for us, which she tried to do for five or seven minutes each time. Each time, several available cabs passed her by. Each time, after about five minutes of not having a cab stop, I (a white woman) would then try to hail one, and within less than a minute or two, a cab would pull up. I was immediately struck by how this had to be explicit bias based on her skin color. She shrugged it off and said, "Welcome to my world. This happens to me and other black people all the time."

Richard Amador, a seasoned employment and business trial lawyer at Sanchez & Amador, LLP, a law firm member of the Minority Corporate Counsel Association, (www.mcca.com), the National Association of Minority & Women Owned Law Firms (https://namwolf.org), and the California Minority Counsel Program (https://cmcp.org), says, "Law firm diversity went backwards in the Great Recession, and I fear it may happen again with the 2020 crisis. Back then, law firms had to cut Diversity & Inclusion programs and reduce headcount, and those cuts hit diverse attorneys hardest."

He continues, "General and in-house counsel can have a *huge* impact on the use of diverse lawyers. They can specifically request diverse associates who have served them well in the past, when assigning matters. They can let law firm relationship partners and practice group leaders know about great results and client service achieved by their diverse associates.

"Law firm partners can make the most direct impact in keeping diverse associates. They can assign diverse associates to important matters and key clients. Provide clear guidance and specific feedback for improvement. Give them more, not less, responsibility now. Check in to make sure their plates are full but that they're not overwhelmed. Ask how they're doing and if they have concerns, then provide honest answers."

> It's important not to let the value
> of diversity become forgotten
> during bad economic times.
> Diversity was a strategic imperative
> when the economy was thriving,
> and it remains so now.
>
> – Sharon E. Jones

Sharon E. Jones, a graduate of both Harvard Law School and Harvard College, is a pioneering supporter of diversity and inclusion in the legal profession. She served as an in-house lawyer in leading corporate legal departments and now serves as CEO of Jones Diversity Inc., where she consults with law firms and legal departments on diversity and inclusion.

She says, "It's important not to let the value of diversity become forgotten during bad economic times. Diversity was a strategic imperative when the economy was thriving, and it remains so now. There are so many excellent resources available online to easily find diverse lawyers, and your ability to recruit them in a downturn may be easier than during an upturn in the market. Consider the following sources, including (but not limited to), the Diversity Committee with your law firm, the Minority Corporate Counsel Association (www.mcca.com), the Black Women Lawyers Association (https://blackwomenlawyers.org), Lawyers of Color (https://lawyersofcolor.org), and the National Association of Women Lawyers (www.nawl.org), among many others."

Here are some additional tips on relationships and communications with people from the book *The Ultimate Women Associates' Law Firm Marketing Checklist* by Ross Fishman, JD and Susan Freeman, MA.

Be Mindful of the Differences in Communication Styles: Growing up, boys and girls are often segregated, restricting them to socialize solely with individuals of their own gender, learning a distinct culture as well as their gender's norms. This results in differences in communication between men and women, inclining both genders to communicate for contrasting reasons. For example, men are more likely to communicate to maintain their status and independence, while women tend to view communication as a path to create friendships and build relationships.

For men, communication is a way to negotiate power, seek wins, avoid failure, and offer advice, among other things. For women, communication is a way to get closer, seek understanding, and find equality or symmetry. Much of this communication takes place using nonverbal cues. More than half (approx. seventy percent) of all communication in conversation is done so in nonverbal form. These same concepts play out in the law firm setting. Being aware and adapting your thinking—and behavior—will help you to succeed with colleagues and clients.

Don't Fall Victim to Stereotypes: Not everyone fits into the generalizations about men and women. Whether it's your genetic makeup or the environment you were raised in, many factors can dictate how you act. People may vary widely from the norms.

Stay Aware: Understand that men and women have different communication styles. Do not be offended when a person of the opposite gender responds or acts in a way different from what you were expecting. There are gender differences in: nonverbal cues; facial expressions; physical space; touch; posture, use of gestures; eye contact; how misunderstandings are overcome; and paralanguage, which is defined as "the non-lexical component of communication by speech, for example intonation, pitch and speed of speaking, hesitation noises, gesture and facial expression"; paralanguage is used by women much more than men.

It's also important to be aware of overall generational differences. For example, most "Veterans" and "Baby Boomers"—those born between approximately 1920-1945 and 1946-1964, respectively—generally work hard, respect or question authority, sacrifice fun for duty/responsibility, put work high on list of priorities, and usually adhere to structure and rules. "Gen Xers" and "Millennials"—those born between 1965-1980 and 1981-2000 respectively, are generally more self-motivated and entrepreneurial; they are goal-oriented and prioritize self-family-personal goals and interests above all else. So, age differences need to be considered and adapted to when communicating or working with people born in different generations.

Key Takeaways

> Embrace the fact that all professional services firms and providers are in the people business, and it is people who hire, retain, use and pay for all professional services.

> Know and embrace the new relationship realities that impact you, clients, employees, and all stakeholders.

> Capture every person (or most people) you meet in an organized manner, preferably automated either by connecting to them on LinkedIn/other social media and/or or obtaining their business card and adding them into your automated contact list.

> Learn and embrace the natural differences in communication styles and preferences.

> Increase your self-knowledge, self-awareness and understanding about your personal style, its strengths and weaknesses.

> Expand diversity and continue to obtain diverse perspectives.

4

OBJECTIVELY ASSESS YOUR NATURAL PERSONAL STYLE AND PREFERENCES

In good economies and bad, a proven path to success is to be aware of and work to regularly improve your strengths, as well as to be aware of and work to minimize your weaknesses.

As described, most highly educated professionals are natural introverts, a style that comes with both strengths as well as weaknesses, when it comes to communicating with people. Introverted people tend to have much less emotional intelligence and empathy than those who are naturally extroverted by nature. Peter Salovey and John Mayer define emotional intelligence as "the ability to monitor one's own and other people's emotions, to discriminate between different emotions and label them appropriately, and to use emotional information to guide thinking and behavior."[25]

Jeff Carr says, "In general, most highly educated professionals score high on the introvert end of the spectrum, so it's not easy for introverts to have an intimate conversation—whether for business or socially."

To increase your emotional intelligence, try approaching the problem backwards. Instead of trying to improve your emotional intelligence skills, strive to identify and eliminate the unconscious habits that are interfering with your natural emotional intelligence in the first place. Try to be conscious of and avoid:

- ✓ Criticizing others
- ✓ Worrying about the future
- ✓ Ruminating on the past
- ✓ Expecting too much of others.[26]

If you have never taken a personal-style analysis or personality test or assessment, now is the time. Doing so can greatly increase your self-knowledge and awareness and enhance your ability to improve your relationships, both professionally and personally.

If you are not familiar with the world-renowned Myers-Briggs Type Indicator® (MBTI) Personality Inventory (Indicator), it was invented by Isabel Briggs Myers and her mother, Katharine Briggs, in the 1940s. The Indicator was designed to make the insights of the theory of psychological types described by C. G. Jung understandable and useful in people's lives.

The MBTI:

1. Identifies basic preferences in each of the four functions in Jung's theory: sensation, intuition, feeling, and thinking; one of these four functions is dominant for a person most of the time.
2. Identifies and describes sixteen distinctive personality types that result from the interactions among the preferences.[27]

The essence of the MBTI is that much seemingly random variation in behavior is quite orderly and consistent, as it is due to basic differences in the ways people tend and prefer to use their perception and judgment.

Isabel Briggs Myers says, "Perception involves all the ways of becoming aware of things, people, happenings, or ideas. Judgment involves all the ways of coming to conclusions about what has been perceived. If people differ systematically in what they perceive and in how they reach conclusions, then it is only reasonable for them to differ correspondingly in their interests, reactions, values, motivations, and skills."

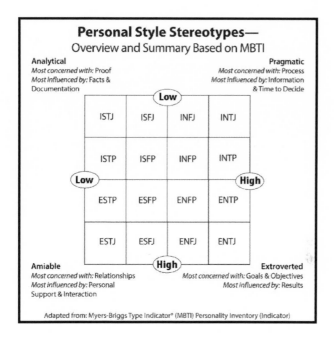

Adapted from: Myers-Briggs Type Indicator® (MBTI) Personality Inventory (Indicator)

If you are not already familiar with the work of Dr. Larry Richard, founder and principal at LawyerBrain, LLC (www.lawyerbrain.com), here is a summary of some of his key findings based on researching thousands of lawyers' natural tendencies and personal styles. His research found that, as compared to the general public, most lawyers are:

- ✓ **Highly skeptical**—defined as cynical, judgmental, questioning, argumentative, and somewhat self-protective.
- ✓ **Naturally antisocial**—defined as having a lack of desire to interact with people, especially when it comes to forming new, intimate connections with others.
- ✓ **Highly autonomous**—defined as resistant to being told what to do, being managed; are highly independent.
- ✓ **Not very resilient**—defined as being hypersensitive to criticism and defensive; they resist taking and accepting feedback.

✓ **In a big hurry/have a strong sense of urgency**—characterized by impatience, a need to get things done, immediacy.[28]

Natural introverts tend to make quick judgments (especially about other people) and tend to overthink; they presume and assume (because they are so highly educated) they already know everything there is to know and what they think is the only possible conclusion. In the current market, this type of mindset and thinking can be detrimental.

Eighty percent of lawyers, along with many other highly educated professionals, are—not surprisingly—heavy thinkers. Being a heavy thinker helps drive the pursuit of excellence in the practice of law, but it can cause issues when communicating with other people.

A key feature of most introverts, high on the Thinking vs. Feeling scale in the MBTI, is egocentricity. A thinker, for example, does not commonly say, "Oh, I see. My colleague (or client or spouse) is using a different decision strategy from me and prefers to evaluate things based on personal preference."

Instead, the thinker is likely to assume that logic applies to everyone and the other person is simply using logic poorly. As a result, thinkers tend to be quick to ignore, dismiss, or minimize the other person's input or perspective. Feelers may do the same thing in reverse, i.e., they may conclude that thinkers are insensitive and out of touch.

Most highly educated people, such as lawyers, accountants, and other professionals, as a group, tend to be strong thinkers and therefore tend to minimize the importance of people's feelings.

As a result, very smart professionals can easily offend people by failing to be sensitive to how people feel (either they are not naturally "warm & fuzzy" or because they may be too blunt). So, soften up a bit, be less self-absorbed, and you will attract more prospective clients to you.

How can smart, highly educated professionals use the thinking/feeling distinction to advantage? Thinkers can learn to recognize which of their colleagues or clients are feelers and make a concerted effort to be more liberal with praise, more judicious with criticism. Feelers can learn to develop a thicker skin and come to realize their more prevalent thinker colleagues mean no harm in offering criticism. In fact, the criticism is usually intended to be helpful.

Because the majority of lawyers and other highly educated professionals are naturally introverted, it is crucial they make a concerted effort to be conscious and understanding of other people's feelings. Granted, this does not come easy to most natural introverts.

Because of these natural/evolved personal and communication styles, most introverts (unless they are involved in a specific, usually obvious, situation, such as when attending a client-centric event) do not readily make an effort to *identify with* others. Instead, their natural tendency is to make an effort to *separate from* others. For example, when in line at a coffee shop or in an elevator, most naturally introverted people do not initiate saying hello to other people (unless they already know them).

Another personal style assessment tool is DISC, a behavior assessment tool based on the DISC theory of psychologist William Moulton Marston. It centers on four different personality traits: Dominance (D), Influence (I), Steadiness (S), and Conscientiousness (C). This theory was later developed into a behavioral assessment tool by industrial psychologist Walter Vernon Clarke.

The chart below, based on the DISC theory, categorizes individual behavioral tendencies into four quadrants. The proven best practice is to use these proven tools to become and stay aware of your own tendencies and way of doing things. Try to anticipate and estimate others' preferences, tendencies, and styles before communicating with others, and make efforts to adapt your style to theirs wherever possible and appropriate.

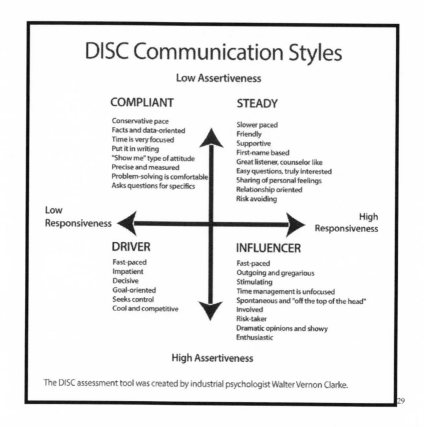

DISC Communication Styles

Low Assertiveness

COMPLIANT

Conservative pace
Facts and data-oriented
Time is very focused
Put it in writing
"Show me" type of attitude
Precise and measured
Problem-solving is comfortable
Asks questions for specifics

STEADY

Slower paced
Friendly
Supportive
First-name based
Great listener, counselor like
Easy questions, truly interested
Sharing of personal feelings
Relationship oriented
Risk avoiding

Low Responsiveness — High Responsiveness

DRIVER

Fast-paced
Impatient
Decisive
Goal-oriented
Seeks control
Cool and competitive

INFLUENCER

Fast-paced
Outgoing and gregarious
Stimulating
Time management is unfocused
Spontaneous and "off the top of the head"
Involved
Risk-taker
Dramatic opinions and showy
Enthusiastic

High Assertiveness

The DISC assessment tool was created by industrial psychologist Walter Vernon Clarke.

Work to understand others' needs and objectives

Every client, referral source, or prospective client has two parallel sets of goals, needs, and desires operating within their minds simultaneously at all times; i.e., everyone has both a business and a personal agenda. Learning and understanding what each consists of cannot be found only through publicly available information. Certainly, the goals and objectives of many companies and organizations can be discerned by researching and studying publicly available information. But with any individual's personal agenda, the only way to learn about it and know is to ask about it at the right time by asking appropriate, strategic, and good questions, and only after a relationship of trust and confidence is established. No one will tell another person or professional what their true goals, needs, and desires are without first having a relationship based on trust and confidence with them.

For example, those who serve in C-suite positions, such as Chief Executive, Financial, or Legal Officers, may have or demonstrate less fear than the average person, simply because they have been forced to face and manage the myriad issues and impacts resulting from the 2020 crisis to date. While also experiencing the personal impact of the 2020 crisis, they have been and will continue to operate and communicate in a businesslike, professional manner.

Whatever personal and professional fears, anxieties, or insecurities they are feeling will often be hidden, not discussed, or even be unconscious to them. All professional service providers need to know and embrace the fact that all people, including all clients, have been and will continue to experience fears related both to their business/organization and to themselves personally. Due to heightened emotions caused by a pandemic, the importance of the client's perspective to how professional services are marketed, sold, communicated, bought, and used has never been greater. Specific strategies and options are described in Chapters 7 and 10.

So, what each individual person/professional does, what we say, and how we act toward all people we come across in every aspect of our life, along with the information we share during and after the 2020 crisis, will be remembered and make an impact. The impact is to your reputation and brand, which has a direct impact on the effectiveness of marketing and business development efforts.

Key Takeaways

> ➢ The need for being empathetic is heightened during a pandemic.
> ➢ Embrace the science (body of knowledge) about personal style and communications.
> ➢ Know your personal style and its strengths and weaknesses (which we all have).

- ➤ Work to maximize your natural strengths and preferences while minimizing the impact of your natural weaknesses.
- ➤ Remember that your perspective is yours alone. Very few people think, act, or view the world/reality in the same way you do.
- ➤ Accept and embrace different styles and perspectives.
- ➤ Each person has their own business and personal motives, values, and agenda, which are hard to fully know and understand.
- ➤ Be aware of the degree of emotion and assertiveness others use when communicating and consider adapting your style as appropriate for each situation.
- ➤ Every single human being you come across in life has the potential, to some degree, to be a referral source. Treat them accordingly.

5

OBJECTIVELY ASSESS YOUR MINDSET

No matter how smart, educated, logical, or reasonable a person is, once a pandemic or another major crisis hits, fear appears, and emotions are felt by all human beings.

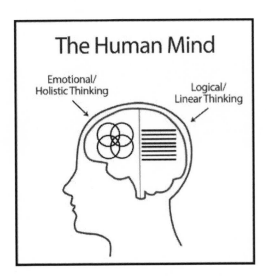

How each person handles their emotions varies at any time, but especially during a crisis. Consider the chart below, which visualizes the answer to the question, "Who do I want to be during 2020 crisis?" Review and objectively assess where you are or were on the chart. If you were not or are not in the "growth zone," consider ways to adapt.

Know that fear will never fully disappear, even when a pandemic or crisis ends. The only thing any human being can fully control is themselves, their own thinking, choices, behavior, and communications. Make sure yours will help build and add to your reputation.

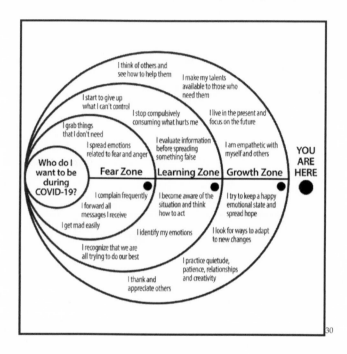

During a pandemic, having tools and techniques to manage personal fear amidst uncertainty is critical. The key is to work to accept, eventually embrace, try to compartmentalize, and ultimately get over your fears as much as is possible.

Overcoming fear, adversity, and trauma is *not* easy. It is a process. Take it from me. Fifteen years ago, I was the victim of several major crimes, all in one day, over six hours, which took me *years* to overcome and recover from. There are many things that helped me manage and move past the post-traumatic stress disorder (PTSD), including regularly writing down/journaling my feelings and thoughts; regularly talking with professionals and friends who were and are supportive; practicing meditation/being fully present; and controlling my thoughts/mind. My PTSD will never fully go away, but the resilience I have built up helped me a lot during the 2020 crisis. How? I would say things to myself like, "At least I don't have a gun pointed at my head" or "I am safe in my own home." "I have a roof over my head and water." "This is not as bad as that," etc.

To overcome fear and maintain personal wellness, there are numerous resources and lots of information on these topics available on LinkedIn and the Internet. Two of the most proven mind-brain tools that help overcome fear are:

1. Practice deep breathing, mindfulness, and meditation regularly.

2. Put all your fears in writing, creating separate lists for personal and professional fears. And do not just put them in writing once. Instead, consider making time to do so regularly (often referred to as journaling). Schedule time to review and think about the items on your list, asking yourself, "What is this fear trying to teach me?" "What can I do to minimize this fear from being realized?" "What can I do to minimize the negative results from this fear?"

3. Then, repeat step 1 above, while saying to yourself, "All I can really and truly control is myself, my thoughts, my own actions, and my behavior and communications."

In your mind, is your glass half empty or half full?

Without being conscious or fully aware of this, many professional services providers have a "glass half empty" mentality; they think mainly about what they do not have. For example, many providers think that new business and opportunities come mainly from people other than their current clients and from contacts or connections they do not yet have. This is a perfect and common example of "glass half empty" thinking.

In fact, most new business and new opportunities come directly or indirectly from existing clients and contacts, either as more work, new types of work, or as word-of-mouth referrals and introductions. So, in fact, most busy professional services providers' glasses are half full, not half empty!

Be (or become) aware of your biases

All human beings have behavioral and communication biases—explicit, implicit, conscious, and unconscious.[31]

In fact, there is a large body of research showing that computerized algorithms are less biased and more accurate than humans.[32]

What is an example of explicit bias? The most obvious example during the 2020 crisis is that many of us are wary of and biased against those who may have the disease and/or all other people we come near, simply because we do not necessarily know who may have the disease or not.

Another example is an explicit bias I experienced professionally. Years ago, after presenting a retreat program to approximately 100 partners of a law firm, the then-managing partner came up to me afterwards and said, "With those eyelashes and that chest, what makes you think I can learn anything from you?"

Over the years, I have had many similar remarks or comments made to me, which essentially are people making judgments about me based on how I look. This often does play against me, since many times, once you are judged based on your looks, few people look past that to understand your capabilities or try to learn about you as a person. This same behavior is aimed even more so at professional women of color than at professional white women like me and is similarly detrimental to their careers.

Fast-forward to today: in this more politically correct world, these types of blatantly sexual and misogynist comments are not verbalized as often anymore, but the thoughts and biases which lead to these types of comments often remain as unconscious or conscious biases within many people's minds.

What is implicit or unconscious bias? It's when our preconceived mindset, attitudes, or stereotypes impact our actions or decisions in an unconscious manner. For example, when a professional only talks to or goes to lunch with people much like themselves; i.e., when a white man only goes to lunch with other white men or a Jewish woman only or mainly talks to other Jewish women. Or, when a person of color or woman talks, their remarks are ignored or minimized. Certainly, these may also be examples of explicit or conscious biases, but most people are not aware of their implicit or unconscious biases.

If you have not gone through conscious and unconscious bias training, now is the time to consider doing so. (Sharon Jones, who was quoted in Chapter 3, provides excellent programs and guidance on these topics.)

Consider whether you may inadvertently exhibit the Dunning-Kruger effect

Do you have and exhibit an overabundance of self-confidence? Do you think you already know everything there is to know about everything else? And/or do you a need to be "the smartest person in the room"? If so, you may have blinders on and will tend not to listen to other, different, or new perspectives.

Many highly educated professionals fall victim to the Dunning-Kruger effect, in which people with low ability at a task or subject overestimate their ability. It is a cognitive bias of illusory superiority that stems from the inability of people to recognize their lack of ability or lack of self-awareness.

As an example, some people criticize Jared Kushner for displaying an overabundance of self-confidence. Because he was a successful businessman does not necessarily mean he is an expert on Middle East relations or anything else in his designated White House portfolio. But *he likely* thinks he is. Whether this is true or not is debatable, but he may suffer from the Dunning-Kruger effect.

The Dunning-Kruger effect plays out regularly in many professional services firms, because many of the fee-earners often think they know more about many things, such as marketing, business development, human resources, etc., and as a result, they dismiss, minimize, or try to stop them.

For example, many providers ignore the need to be active on professionally relevant social media platforms, like LinkedIn. Their thinking is, "All my business comes from relationships, so being active on LinkedIn is a waste of my time." Yet, LinkedIn has the greatest global business-to-business (B2B) reach of any media, and it does not cost much to use. Professionals who minimize its importance are missing out on its power and reach.

Consider whether you are an "intellectual piranha." What is an intellectual piranha? A highly educated professional trained to identify and eliminate, avoid, overcome, manage, or minimize risk, who has the (often unconscious) tendency to verbally or otherwise critique and tear apart new ideas and different perspectives. In a post-pandemic world, being an intellectual piranha could be a detriment and threat to survival and future success.

Are you "solutions" or "practice" focused?

At all times, clients want answers and solutions to their problems, and they want them as quickly, efficiently, in as high quality, and as cost-effectively as possible. Clients do not really care about the internal politics and operating issues of any outside firms with whom they work. They care mainly about what they receive from the firms and providers they hire and use.

A solution-oriented approach is client-centric. It recognizes:

1. Clients have a preference for demonstrable innovation that creates value by being better/faster/cheaper and delivers insights that create more business value.

2. Clients have constraints generated by their business requirements, which drives reduced-rate pressure on outside professional services providers.

3. Clients are increasingly building up in-house talent and solution capabilities, which is major competition for outside service providers.

4. Clients are unbundling services by stripping off work that used to fill the buy basket, introducing competition lower in the complexity stack, and creating disruptive potential.[33]

5. Regulatory barriers are melting.

6. The pace of technological change is increasing and development costs are dropping.[34]

Are you a "giver"?

The best way to establish and build successful relationships is to give useful, helpful advice, introductions, opportunities, and even suggestions of great movies or shows. Being a giver is a proven path to a successful career. In fact, many of the world's most successful rainmakers focus on helping others in many ways, both personally and professionally. Familiar sayings include, "Give to get" and "What goes around, comes around."

In the "serving people" business, which all professionals are in, reciprocal relationships are the best and most fruitful.

We are each the "center of the universe" in our own world. But every client and every other person's "center of the universe" is different. Some friends, family, and/or colleagues may have similar priorities as yours, but you know only a small percentage of those. Avoid being a professional who sits, waits, takes, hopes, and expects opportunities to fall into your lap.

Sincere, authentic interest in clients and contacts is critical to developing new business. All clients have work, family, hobbies, interests, unrealized dreams, aspirations, and bucket lists. Learn what is important to your clients/contacts and what issues they are facing (both professionally and personally, as appropriate). Focusing on other people and their needs will bring you closer to fulfilling yours. Again, not what you *think* they might like or find valuable, but what you *know* they would value and like, based on your knowledge and understanding of them, their organization, needs, objectives, and desires. If you do not know, ask "Would you like X?" or "If we did Y, would you find it valuable?", etc.

Some questions to ask yourself:

1. What would my contact/client/person find helpful, useful and/or of interest?

2. What do they like? What are they interested in/motivated by?

3. What will make them happy(ier) and/or more successful? Look good? Feel good?

Consider what you can proactively offer or do that would enhance your relationship and add value to the client's or contact's business or personal life. Such as: offering no-charge or discounted services; technology options or monitoring services; tailored presentations/CLE for their team; research; secondments, introductions, access, invitations, tips for new restaurants, etc.

Trust is a foundation to a successful practice and firm

We all know that every professional services firm operates best and that related professional services are delivered best when relationships are grounded in trust and confidence. This includes both internal and external relationships with clients and other stakeholders.

Trust is defined as a reliance on character, ability, strength, or a combination of these traits, and one in which confidence is placed. The legendary consultant to professional services firms David Maister (now retired) came up with an equation for trust:

Trust = IC²RS/Self

Self = Demonstrating a Low Level of Self by Minimizing Own Ego and Sense of Superiority

Interest in Them

Care and Concern

Credible & Reliable & Sincere

A client's trust needs to be earned. Once you do that, the result will not just be a happy client; they will be a client for life.

What does it take to earn a client's trust? Here are some examples:

- Telling clients they are better off not pursuing a matter or case.
- Telling clients things they do not necessarily want to hear.
- Telling the client you or your firm cannot handle something and offering to help them find another resource or professional.
- Owning up to your mistakes (e.g., overruns or unnecessary work).
- Rigorously keeping the client's confidences.
- Praising the work of another firm.
- Advising clients proactively of things they could be doing more efficiently or in-house.[35]

Here are some ways to build, develop and increase trust:

- Engage/reach out—do not wait for clients/contacts to reach out to you
- Listen—the power goes to those who ask and listen, not those who argue and persuade.
- Restate, summarize, and frame—e.g., "So, I understand you want to know whether your general liability policy might cover

business interruption costs. Is that right?" "Is that your only policy?"

- Envision the outcome, what is next, and verbalize it (or draft a brief proposal in writing).

- Commit to staying in touch—schedule reminders and false deadlines (see discussion, Chapter 10) to force yourself to initiate contact.

Trusting your partners and staff

Many lawyers and other professionals remain distrustful of their partners, colleagues, and others. This is partially due to the natural, introverted personal style of most highly educated professionals (see Chapter 4).

Most professional services firms (like many other businesses) have layers of internal politics (caused by people, interactions, and communications), which can often lead to emotional insecurity-, fear-, power-, or ego-driven decisions that are not necessarily best for the entire firm.

Many professional services firms are not organized as hierarchies, so decision-making and compliance is often horizontal, i.e., every (or a select few) equity partner has equal power and the complete freedom to choose exactly how they will practice, what resources they will or will not use, and what firm policies they will opt into and comply with. This reality tends to make any "top-down" initiatives coming from firm leadership less than effective and dilutes the firm's culture, cohesion, collaboration, camaraderie, and, most importantly, the realized return on investment from strategic choices and investments.

There is often little or no consequence or penalty for equity partners opting out or not complying with firm directives and policies. As a result, firms in which every partner can do whatever they want are really just "hotels." In other words, each partner is an individual business unit with complete discretion on how to run and operate their practice, no matter the impact on the firm as a whole. There is little "glue" that holds the partnership together, which is a major threat to the firm's survival.

One example is that many professional services firms claim to have a "no a-hole" policy and rule in place—a firm policy that suggests no "a-holes" will be tolerated in the firm and will be "managed" out. But the reality is much different. Most firms have powerful partners who control large books of business via origination credits. Many powerful partners remain resistant to change for numerous reasons. Some can be difficult to work with; they look down upon and are mean to staff members or are bullies, they kibosh any idea that is new or different; or they are otherwise culturally disruptive to the firm. In the wake of the 2020 crisis, will the tolerance level lessen for such bad actors and anyone who weakens camaraderie, firm culture, and the results from strategic investments?

Like "brand", the word "culture" is also hard to define with precision, because it is intangible and amorphous. The only tangible *glue* that may hold a firm together could be its physical offices or technology. The rest of what defines a firm's culture is sustained and developed by people, a camaraderie between the people who work for and with the firm.

Any firm's culture consists mainly of a feeling and a way of doing business and behaving. Some law firms without a strong and well-defined culture are often referred to as "hotels for lawyers," which may be one cause of lateral turnover. Read more about what defines firm culture here: https://abovethelaw.com/2020/05/what-is-the-definition-of-a-law-firm/.

Caitlin (Cat) Moon, is the Director of Innovation Design, Vanderbilt Law School, Program on Law & Innovation, the Director of Design the Law Lab, and an instructor of radiology at Vanderbilt University Medical School. She suggests, "Now, more than ever, the world needs empathetic lawyers and providers who are capable of putting themselves in their clients' shoes, seeing the world from clients' perspective, and tailoring their counsel accordingly. Many already do this. Those who thrive in the post-crisis world most certainly will do this."

How might you embrace these superpowers to design how and what you do to best serve clients, during a crisis and beyond?

- **Curiosity**: Ask lots of questions before you start giving answers. Listen more than you talk. Exhibit humble curiosity by embracing the truth that you will never know all you need to know about anything. Exhibit authentic curiosity about clients and their situations as the foundation for all you do. The best problem-solving starts with humble curiosity about the problem.

- **Empathy**: See clients' challenges from their perspective, and tailor your services accordingly. Seeing a problem from the client's perspective differs from seeing it from the lawyer's perspective. If you problem-solve and communicate only from your perspective, you cannot be client-centered. And, clients don't need lawyer-centered solutions. They need client-centered solutions. This demands empathy.[36]

- **Radical collaboration:** Collaborate with clients and other professionals to develop holistic solutions. "Legal" and other "problems" exist within a wider set of business challenges and issues your clients face. How are you helping clients holistically by truly collaborating with them and other experts to create holistic solutions?

- **Embrace ambiguity:** We all live in a world full of unknowns, more so at this moment than likely anytime in our lives. In this crisis, there is much we simply can't know right now. There are many possible futures, based on factors completely outside of our control. How might you embrace this and lead from it, rather than denying this reality? How might you develop a deeper comfort level with ambiguity, and leverage this to differentiate yourself from those who won't? Because many won't embrace this new normal.

- **Let go of the fear of failure:** Experimenting to create value (i.e., innovation) is demanded by the new normal. We have no choice in this moment but to do things we've never done before, simply to maintain our professional existence. When you can push through the seemingly innate fear of imperfection to experiment with new ways of working and serving clients, your world will expand exponentially. In this moment, "the way we've always done it" doesn't work. We have no choice but to try new ways and learn from what works and what doesn't. When you can execute smart, intentional experiments and learn from them, you will elevate your work and your ability to serve clients with excellence.

Key Takeaways

> ➤ Embrace and learn to control your fears.
> ➤ Work to adopt a growth mindset.
> ➤ View your world and firm as a glass half full.
> ➤ Increase your self-awareness and work to become less self-centric.
> ➤ Become aware of your biases and work to overcome them.
> ➤ Avoid falling victim of the Dunning-Kruger effect.
> ➤ Increase your focus on solutions, which is what all clients want.
> ➤ Be more of a giver rather than a taker.
> ➤ Work to enhance the level of trust in all your relationships.
> ➤ Do more to build and enhance your firm culture.

6

OBJECTIVELY ASSESS YOUR USE OF TIME

At all times, the efficient use of time, especially non-billable time, is crucial to every successful professional. We each only have the same twenty-four hours in each day. So, do the math for yourself and analyze the results.

The Average, Annual Professional Time Breakdown for an Individual Practitioner

52 Weeks in Each Year:

> **Minus 7 Weeks** (for continuing education/vacation/holidays/sick days, etc.) = **45 Weeks**
>
> **45 Weeks x 60** (average work hours per week) = **2,700 Total Hours** (average total per year)

For those on alternative tracks:

> **45 Weeks x 40 Hours/week = 1,800 Hours Total (average Per Year**
>
> **60 Hours Each Week** for *Work* (both billable & non-billable time):
>
> > **2,700 Total Hours** billable & non-billable time, which means, on average, each professional has approximately:
> >
> > **900 "Extra" Hours Annually** = **20** "extra" hours per week
> >
> > **250 Hours Annually** is the average time practitioners devote/invest annually on *business & client development*, which is, on average, **5.5 hours per week** (or approximately **27%** of available non-billable time).

Several studies show that the majority of non-billable time devoted to marketing and business development is spent trying to generate new work from brand-new clients and simply "asking for the business." This is a common mistake. Most lawyers devote very little time researching, analyzing, planning, and preparing opportunities, nor do they spend time conducting private or face-to-face needs-assessment conversations, both of which are critical steps in an effective client development/sales process and program.

- Approximately seventy percent of this time (175 hours annually, four hours per week) is spent/invested in *non-contact activities,* such as: preparing for and speaking, writing, attending, etc. designed to generate opportunities from brand-new or existing clients (i.e., glass half full thinking, as described in Chapter 5).

- Approximately thirty percent of this time (75 hours annually or 1.65 hours weekly) is spent/invested in *direct, face-to-face, small group or one-to-one communications* with clients, contacts/prospects, after which approximately ninety-five percent of new business is awarded/obtained.

Work to optimize your use of your professional time to increase your productivity

Some questions about your use of your professional time to ask yourself:

- ✓ How do I currently use/invest my non-billable and "extra" time?
- ✓ What are my professional and career goals and priorities?
- ✓ Do I devote my time in alignment with them?
- ✓ Where do I "waste" the most time?
- ✓ Could my non-billable time be used more effectively?
- ✓ What is my highest and best use?
- ✓ What am I best at?
- ✓ What work do I enjoy doing the most?

✓ What is my greatest contribution/value-add?

✓ What do I spend time on that can be leveraged to someone else, whether an internal staff member or outsourced?

✓ On a daily basis, ask yourself, "What is the most valuable use of my time, right now?"

Lack of time is the greatest challenge all professionals face

Most of a fee-earner's total available professional time is spent producing and delivering work to clients. All firms' revenues are generated by fee-earners and professionals producing, delivering, billing for, and collecting on the work they do for clients. So, most spend eighty to a hundred percent of their time fueling the lifeblood of the firm by generating billable hours and revenues. Due to these realities, once fee-earners are done with the substantive work and associated tasks, most are either exhausted or have numerous other professional and personal demands on their remaining available time.

The bad news:

Effective and efficient use of time is nothing but a discipline. It takes hard work, dedication, consistency, and self-awareness. Even for those who are highly disciplined time managers, it is not easy to do 100% of the time. Especially when a pandemic or crisis hits, every person gets waylaid from their original plans when other more urgent and important things take precedence.

Most professional services providers, especially those who work under a billable-hour model have numerous demands on their time and find they have very little time left in any given day, week, or month to create and implement an effective business development program (or to devote time to other non-urgent but important projects and tasks).

Even those professional services providers who find or make the time to create a marketing/business development plan often find they have little time to implement the tactics of the program, such as writing articles, obtaining speaking engagements, doing social media posts, etc.

The good news:

There are proven technology options and tricks that can really help you allocate, manage, and use your time most productively, efficiently, and effectively.

For example, almost all professionals use some sort of automated calendar such as Outlook, Google, Apple, or iCloud calendars. But many do not use it optimally, nor do they coordinate with their staff members to optimize its use. Most lawyers and other professional services providers are largely reactive, i.e., mainly responding to calls, emails, and attending to the urgent and important things they need to get done each day.

If you have not read *The 7 Habits of Highly Effective People* by Stephen Covey, I highly recommend it. It changed my life for the better. Below is a key chart in the book that demonstrates how work that is important but not urgent rarely gets done because eighty to a hundred percent of working hours are taken up by getting all the urgent things done (some of which are important, but not all).

How can you make time for those critical tasks that are important but not urgent? Tasks like planning, relationship check-ins, upgrades to technology, training, coaching, mentoring, business development, and professional development are all examples of tasks that are important but not necessarily urgent (unless the deadline for completing required continuing education to report to your licensing body is fast approaching; then, getting your CE is urgent and important, because, if you don't, your license or certification will be suspended!).

Effective Time Management Matrix

Important

Urgent	Not Urgent
Crises	Preparation/Prevention
Pressing Problems	Planning/Strategizing
Deadline-Driven Projects,	Relationship Building
Meetings, Preparations	Recognizing New Opportunities
	Prediction Improvements
	Rejuvenation

Not Important

Urgent	Not Urgent
Interruptions	Busy Work, Trivia
Some Mail/Reports	Some Mail, Phone Calls
Some Meetings	Time Wasters
Pressing, Proximate Matters	Pleasant Activities
Popular Activities	"Escape" Activities

Source: Seven Habits of Highly Effective People by Stephen Covey

Few professionals use their automated calendar in a disciplined manner to proactively schedule time each day, week, month, or quarter to attend to business and client development efforts. Nor do they use it to schedule reminders to do things that are important but not urgent. Instead, they rely on their memory to remind them.

Natural and learned rainmakers and professional salespeople create and commit to a schedule or routine regarding their marketing and business development. But most other professional services providers do not. Instead, they just think about or do MBDCS efforts when they remember to, when work is slow, or when they happen to find some extra time.

The difference between being *interested* versus being *committed* to something is vast. When you are simply interested in something, you don't necessarily take it seriously. You pay attention to it only when it occurs to you or when something prompts or reinvigorates your interest (such as you know your annual contribution report will be due soon, for compensation purposes). But when you are committed, you do everything it takes to be sure you get it done—no distraction or excuse stops you; you do it no matter what.

For example, if you are committed to staying in shape, you do not simply work out when it occurs to you or when you find some "extra" time. Instead, you are likely committed to it by having a schedule and routine that you make yourself adhere to most of the time. If a distraction arises, you do your best to put it aside to address after your workout. You make a concerted effort to plan your schedule to allow for working out. Staying in shape is an example of a commitment made possible purely and only by self-discipline.

The same type of commitment needs to be applied to your work. Establishing a disciplined use of your automated calendar for proactive scheduling takes you out of the vortex of being ninety to a hundred percent reactive in your work, helps you avoid being a slave to the demands of the day, and instead allows you to be routinely reminded to dedicate time to all your important yet not urgent tasks and projects, such as implementing relevant business development tactics.

A proven best practice used by many successful practitioners is to set up meetings and appointments with themselves in their automated calendar. Doing so carves out and makes time to be proactive and attend to work that is important but not necessarily urgent.

So, consider creating regular reminders for yourself using auto-recurring Outlook/calendar meetings or appointments with yourself and any relevant staff members. Once set, they automatically pop into your calendar each day/week/month or year, so you do not have to rely on your memory alone. Remember: no matter how educated or smart a person is, relying on memory alone is not reliable, and misses details and nuances that are important in all relationships.[37]

Automated recurring meetings or reminders can also be set up verbally using the assistance of Siri, Alexa, or Google Assistant on mobile devices. The how-tos vary depending on which automated calendar system you use. Ask your assistant or IT (information technology) professional for assistance.

Schedule these recurring meetings with yourself for ten minutes to an hour once a week (ideally), and use that time to stop, reflect, think of your key clients and contacts, and ask yourself:

- What is new, developing, or coming up for this key contact (either professionally or personally)? Do I know? If you do not know for sure or are assuming you already know, ask them.

- What problems or issues are they facing lately? Do I know? Or am I assuming or presuming?

- What else could I be doing or delivering to this key contact? What additional value could my firm and I provide?

More resources on contact analysis can be found in Appendixes 2 and 3.

A related best practice is to draft a list of the key people in your professional life *in writing*, then insert it into your recurring calendar meetings with yourself. This practice helps ensure you stay in touch, maintain, and develop your key relationships without having to rely on your memory alone.

I call these types of key contact lists or pipelines "Money Books" or "Success Books," because without these key people/professionals, you would not have a successful practice.

For example, list:

1. Your assistant and all other internal support staff whom you rely on and call upon to get your work done.

2. The leader of your departments, practice areas, and any other relevant firm leaders.

3. Your top five to ten internal colleagues who refer work to you or have done so in the past.

4. Your top five to ten existing clients

5. Your top three to five external referral sources. (If you do not have any yet, list possible, potential future referral sources such

as a college, graduate, and law school classmates or family members.)

6. The top vendors or outside consultants you hire, use, and work with to get work done

7. Your top three to five prospective clients (e.g., maybe someone you went to school with works at a company where you think the firm could provide professionals services for in the future).

8. Your top five to ten past, nonactive clients and referral sources, those whom you may have worked for in the past but have not stayed in touch with.

9. Those who are in a position to refer work to you, but you have never raised the issue or asked them.

If you need assistance to create your Money/Success Book or to set automatically recurring reminders in your online calendar, ask your assistant, an internal staff member, or an external coach for help.

Key Takeaways

➤ Embrace the fact that time management is a discipline that takes never-ending work and effort.

➤ Analyze your use of your professional time.

➤ Decide what you are most committed to accomplishing/working on.

➤ Determine what upgrades, changes would make better use of your time and make you more productive.

➤ Increase your time management and self-discipline as needed.

➤ Make better use of your automated calendar, setting reminders, etc.

➤ Create and use a "Money/Success Book" list, and insert it into your weekly meetings with yourself.

- ➢ When the meeting pops up in your calendar, review your "Money Book" list and make appropriate outreaches during that time.
- ➢ Leverage your time by asking for and obtaining assistance for non-critical work or for tasks that can be done by others.

7

OBJECTIVELY ASSESS YOUR KNOWLEDGE, UNDERSTANDING & EXPECTATIONS

What do you know, understand, and expect regarding the business development, marketing, client development (sales), and client service (MBDCS) processes?

For both firms and individual practitioners, marketing, business development, and communications (MBDCS) investments and efforts take on much greater strategic importance during economic downturns. So, optimizing them is essential to survive and thrive in the future.

All professional services firms and providers face similar challenges to effective MBDCS, especially since all firms and practitioners have a limited budget and a limited amount of time to invest.

> To survive and thrive, all lawyers, firms, and other professionals must continue to invest in strategic marketing, selling, and related communications. Few firms or individual professionals without an effective marketing and sales program ever survive economic disruptions.
>
> – Ralph Baxter

Define your *Brand*

The word "brand" is often perceived as an amorphous and intangible phrase. Yet, every professional services firm and individual practitioner already has a brand. What is it? Your brand is:

* An authentic representation of who you are in the minds of others, from their perspective.

* The words, adjectives, or descriptors that people think of when they hear your firm name or your name, which are referred to as brand attributes or definitions.

* What you are known for in the marketplace and what is said about you and your firm.

Whether you have formally defined your brand or not, you already have one. For example, there are some professional services firms notoriously known as "cut-throat," "sweatshop," "sharks," "white shoe," etc. There are individual practitioners known, talked about, (and therefore branded) as "the go-to professional on X" or "you want Y done, call Z," etc.

If you do not know what defines you and your firm, now is a good time to learn. Not just from your own self-centric or internal perspective, but from your client's perspective. How? By asking a representative sample of your clients, "When you think of me and my services, what adjectives come to mind?"

One thing that helps define the brand of every professional services firm and practitioner is their website. Having a mobile-friendly website that is easy to navigate and use, plus an online biographical sketch rich with relevant up-to-date and useful information, both in writing and visually (i.e., videos) is absolutely essential in this day and age. Yet, most firms never ask or survey their clients and website users what is working and not regarding their website, nor what information and in what format would be most useful to them in website biographical sketches. Instead, the content is created mainly from the internal or self-perspective.

This is a major mistake because almost all potential clients and referral sources do the same thing when they need to or think of using a new lawyer or other new professional services provider: they Google (or use another search engine to search) their name. A major mistake on most firm's website is that there is a lack of a well-defined, market-facing position (often referred to as positioning strategy), especially for practice areas, groups or departments. This makes most firm's website and web presence less than optimal and indistinguishable from competitors.[38]

Your firm name or logo can be put on any tangible item, such as your building, lobby walls, cups, swag, etc. But, after a pandemic, think carefully before branding crisis-related items such as face masks, hand-sanitizing stations, etc., because many may not appreciate or like it. A private poll on Facebook found that many people thought having firm logos on face masks would be off-putting or distasteful.

Your tag line (if you have and use one)

Almost all companies, firms, and other organization have a tag line on their website that defines them or describes what makes them different or better. But these written words are useless to reinforce or build the brand, unless most people (clients, referral sources, prospective clients and referral sources, vendors, etc.) who interact with members of the firm experience those brand attributes. So, the key to your brand is you and each and every person who works for the firm in any capacity. Every day, each of the firm's employees either builds, adds to, or detracts from the firm's brand, word-of-mouth, and reputation, as result of every communication they make. (See Chapter 3.)

For example, there are several major leading firms who have spent (likely) hundreds of thousands of dollars to formally define their brand, creating tag lines such as, "Building a Better Working World"; "When Results Count"; "It's Not a Common Practice"; "Our Mission is Your Success"; "Aspiration Meets Innovation." The list goes on and on.

A written tag line is meaningless and largely worthless, if it is not made tangible. The primary tangible brand-builders for all firms and practices are those things that people can see, touch, and personally experience, such as your website, how you dress, your office, your firm's online platforms, etc. But these tangible things impact less than fifty percent of your brand, image and reputation.

In some cases, the behavior and communications of some members of the firm do not reflect well or improve upon the stated firm brand. For example, at least a dozen different times over the course of my career, I have personally witnessed (or been the recipient of) blatantly dismissive and rude behavior toward me or others by leading members and C-suite executives of major professional services firms. This condescending behavior is usually the result of quick judgments or the fact they have not met a person/do not know them.

Unprofessional, rude, or demeaning behavior reflects badly on firms who allow it. In fact, studies show those who have a negative experience with a firm or company tell an average of fifteen people about it, while only eleven people, on average, tell about a good experience.[39] As a result of my negative experiences with some practitioners from certain firms, when I have an opportunity to refer clients or work to law firms or other professional services firm, I make it a point not to mention or email those firms as options.

Not all fee-earners, executives, and staff realize and embrace the fact that they are each walking/talking/living **brand ambassadors** of their firm, always. They do not embrace the fact they are in the business of serving people, and every interaction with another person either enhances their brand and reputation or diminishes it.

One never knows where the next piece of business will come from or who will be a referral source, so being rude and dismissive toward anyone not only narrows your market, but also dilutes your reputation, brand, and image. For example, years ago, I was working for a leading law firm in New York City, and one of the lawyers with whom I was coaching said to me, "Julie, you will never believe who just referred me to the largest hedge fund in Brazil!"

I replied, "Awesome. Who referred you?"

He said, "A paralegal who just started working at our firm a few weeks ago. It turns out her brother manages one of the largest hedge funds in Brazil."

I asked him if he had asked the paralegal why she referred her brother to him (out of all the other lawyers in the firm). He had not and asked me to do so. So I stopped by her desk and asked, "Can you tell me why you told X (name of lawyer) about your brother's company and told your brother about X?"

She replied, "Because he is the only lawyer who says good morning or hello to me each time I pass him, and he seems like a nice person."

So, how you treat others matters and has a direct impact on your ability to attract referrals and new business.

The most important tangible brand-builder: how people experience you and your firm.

Your brand is a living thing, which is supported or damaged every day, by every interaction, touchpoint, and communication. So, the most important element of building a brand is consistency in all communication. I.e., alignment and integrity between what people experience and what is written on your website/communicated is the key to an effective and long-lasting brand.

Once people experience you and your firm, based on all their touchpoints and interactions, they develop an opinion and perspective on you, your firm, and what they think and feel about both. Their thoughts drive their communications and word of mouth. If they had a positive experience overall, they will be more inclined to speak highly of you. If they were less than fully satisfied and happy with the results, deliverables, and service they received, they will be even more likely to say negative things about you.

Unless you are a practitioner at a large professional services firm, investing in formally defining your brand is probably not the best use of your limited resources. Very few solo practitioners, small, or mid-size professional services firms have enough money and resources to invest in a meaningful, formal branding exercise that will generate measurable results or return on investment.

The most effective and simple way to define your brand is to answer these questions:

- Being true to myself, what do I want to be known and remembered for?

- What do I want former clients, referral sources, and others to say about me/my firm?

- What is my mission, and what are my values?

Excellent or positive experiences and interactions are the best ways for firms and practitioners to unleash and increase positive word of mouth.

Consider working with all members of your firm to educate them on the fact that they are each brand ambassadors for the firm at all times and how important each and every one of their interactions is to help build, increase, or harm your brand, reputation, and the flow of new business and opportunities.

Remember: your brand (as defined by other people) permeates everything you do, everything you communicate, and all your MBDCS investments and efforts.

The business development process for professional services firms defined

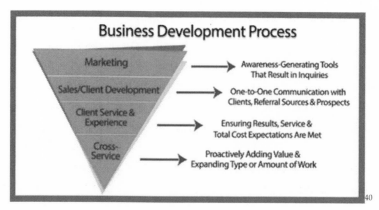

Within most firms, the actual and agreed-upon meanings or definitions of the words marketing, business development, client development, practice development, sales, and related terms are often used interchangeably, and each person's understanding of these terms varies considerably, especially what each term means on a practical, operational, and grassroots level.

The difference between marketing and sales is a lot like the difference between being a general practitioner and an intellectual property litigator—those are two quite different practices and require vastly differing (yet related) bodies of knowledge and capability. Sure, general practitioners can *say* they can handle patent litigation, but do they have the necessary specialized knowledge and ability? The same contrast applies to years of experience—a patent litigator with five years of experience likely does not have the capabilities of one with twenty-five years of experience.

It is a question of semantics. For example, when one says "marketing" to an individual professional, depending upon his or her mindset and knowledge, that person may define marketing narrowly in his or her mind, thinking that media exposure, seminars, blogs, social media, or some combination are what marketing means. Other professionals and attorneys may use the phrase "marketing" to convey their understanding of what business development means to them. Not only do the same words have different meanings within a firm, but most professionals and lawyers also think of marketing as common sense, haphazard, and unpredictable, when in fact, just like civil procedure, business development, marketing, client development/sales, and client service are each a process that is part science, and consist of somewhat linear and predictable steps and yield results when well executed.

These varying differences in the meaning and understanding of business development, marketing, client/development/sales, and client service create a host of issues and challenges within most law firms, especially relating to exactly what firm leaders expect from their in-house marketing/business development staff before and after hiring them. Ralph Baxter says, "Business development/marketing is underutilized in many firms, either out of a lack of understanding of how it works or a lack of confidence in the team. Yet, effective marketing in some form is critical to generating a healthy flow of work in the future."

Many firms and practitioners also continue to make the mistake of "throwing a person at the problem" (the "problem" being MBDCS support), i.e., they hire a full-time MBDCS staff member then expect that one, single professional to get every MBDCS project and task done *and* report measurable results from each. This approach is naive and unrealistic, because it takes *considerable* time, effort, skill, and attention to detail to get most MBDCS and client service initiatives, programs, and communications completed and delivered in a high-quality manner, especially ones that generate the desired results (e.g., qualified leads and actual, measurable new business).

Another common mistake and misconception about MBDCS is the lack of an understanding that most common MBDCS tools and approaches used by firms and practitioners consist of cumulative and step-by-step processes, with many related processes and sub-processes.

Examples of common MBDCS projects or activities that are, in fact, step-by-step processes include:

- Responding to a Request for Proposal/Qualifications (RFP/Q)

- Preparing for new business "pitch" meetings

- Attending a conference or seminar

Process maps for many of these are contained in my book, *Master-Level Business Development Activity Checklists for Lawyers, Law Firms, and Other Professional Services Providers*, available on Amazon. Find more info on the discipline of process mapping in Chapter 10.

Other ways to enhance and improve these critical MBDCS processes are described later, in Chapter 10.

There is a need for a better, more common understanding about MBDCS as it applies to professional services. Why? Because defining and understanding key words and phrases the same way allows all professionals to be on the same page, which creates a better foundation upon which to make strategic decisions and choices in the face of limited budgets and time. Based on my thirty years of professional experience, below are the definitions and meanings of some of the most important and commonly misunderstood MBDCS-related words and phrases.

Definition of *business development* as it applies to professional services

As described in previous chapters of this book, all professional services firms and individual practitioners are in the business of serving people, and people are the most important thing to any firm or practitioner. So, "business development" is and should be thought of as the overarching objective of any firm or practitioner. Why?

Because without business (which is awarded by people), there is no work to do for and deliver to anyone, and there is no one to pay for your professional services. So "business development" is the overarching imperative for every firm and practitioner to even be able to operate (and hence be successful, survive, and thrive). Business development is manifested by everything you or your colleagues do, say, deliver, or communicate, in all aspects of your practice. So, there is an element of business development in *every* aspect of *any* practice and firm.

Definition of *marketing* as it applies to professional services

At the moment, there are approximately 7.6 billion people in the world, a vast number. Very few professional services firms define them all as their market, and few have the budget or resources to effectively market to 7.6 billion people. This vast market of 7.6 billion people is the target market for global mega-brands, such as Microsoft, Google, Amazon, Coca-Cola, Procter & Gamble, Nestlé, etc., who have the resources, scope, and scale to effectively market to 7.6 billion people.

No firm or practitioner can be all things to all people, and trying to do so often results in unproductive, unfocused marketing investments. So, the first and most important marketing strategic task for every firm and practitioner is to precisely define your target market(s).

How? By sorting, sifting, segmenting, and eliminating from the primary market of 7.6 billion people. Target markets and clients should be precisely identified (in writing and by key source) by location, geography, industry, type of problem/matter or case type, type of business, life-cycle stage, size, any combination of these, and any other relevant qualifying factors, which vary for each firm, practice, office, and practitioner. For specific ways to define your target market(s), see Appendix 1.

Once your target market(s) is defined in writing, the next step is to create or find a list of those businesses, organizations, and people in each. These target lists should be reviewed and qualified, as the focus of all (or the vast majority of) your MBDCS investments and efforts, and then tracked.

Without tracking efforts and results, you will never be certain as to what MBDCS efforts work best and which do not. The need to regularly review and assess all MBDCS investments, including staff, is a business discipline many firms and practitioners let fall by the wayside, yet is critical to consistently obtaining a strong return on investment from all your MDBCS investments and efforts.

The primary objective or goal of any marketing tool is to create awareness of the firm and its capabilities in the minds of decision-makers within the relevant target market—usually by deploying commonly used marketing tools such as websites, e-alerts, public relations/media coverage, articles, seminars, social media posts, and speeches.

> The goal of marketing is to create awareness of the firm and its capabilities in the minds of decision-makers within the relevant target market that leads to an inquiry.
>
> – Julie Savarino

Most of these marketing tools are *non-contact* in nature; when seeing/hearing/or otherwise being exposed to the tool, the decision-maker does not necessarily have direct, in-person contact with a member of the firm, particularly not with the partner/attorney capable of handling his or her types of matters. However, to be effective and measurable, all non-contact marketing tools should be designed to lead to a direct, personal contact (aka. a qualified lead) with a firm fee-earner or representative who knows how to engage in the client-relationship development process.

The ultimate goal of any and all marketing tools, then, is and should be to produce a *qualified lead* via direct, personal contact—either by telephone, e-mail, video, or face-to-face with an individual practitioner or attorney.

So, the definition of marketing for professional services is deploying the right mix of messages using tools designed to create awareness about the firm and its capabilities in the minds of target-market decision-makers to generate an inquiry or lead from one or more of them.

To be effective, marketing messages need to be delivered and absorbed by the target audience every thirty to ninety days. This messaging cadence is how to stay "top of mind." The strategy is to deliver similar messaging approximately nine times in nine different ways over time, to generate the awareness that yields a consistent flow of inquires or leads. These inquiries or leads usually come in the form of a phone call, email, or direct message.

Ask yourself how effective your firm's or your own select mix of marketing tools is in attaining these objectives. If you do not formally review and assess your marketing tools and mix at least once each year or two, I encourage you to start doing so, since money and time are limited and all marketing investments need to be optimized.

For example, many practitioners and firms spend considerable time and money creating and producing seminars, articles, podcasts and webinars, yet most make the mistake of not converting spoken content into written form. They do not leverage and re-use the content for other purposes. Yet, all live presentations, webinars, and podcasts can be recorded, transcribed, and then repurposed into blogs, alerts, checklists and social media. This is the type of content clients find useful and in the format they most prefer (because many clients are visual learners). Firms that do not practice this waste a lot of time, resources and miss a significant part of the market (the majority of people who prefer to get new information by seeing or reading it).

Definition of *client development/sales* in professional services firms

Instead of using the word "sales" in the professional services firm environment (which can convey an impression of solicitation, which is unethical for many practitioners and can be considered unprofessional and off-putting to clients and prospects), I prefer to refer to sales in professional services environments as *client development*.

Why? Because all firms seek to develop relationships with clients (people). And consistently developing quality new business for all professional services providers is a *process*, one that takes considerable time, focus, patience, skill, persistence, systems, processes, and procedures to implement successfully and cost-effectively. This sales or client-development process begins and ends with in-person or face-to-face contacts with one person or a small group of individuals (i.e., decision-makers, board members, and influencers).

In fact, studies I have done over the course of my career show that approximately seventy to ninety percent of all new, high-end professional services business is awarded during or shortly after face-to-face meetings with one person or a small group of people (not including plaintiff-side law firms and work won via government or non-profit RFPs).

Wondering whether this statistic applies to your firm or practice? Consider how many times in the past a prospective new client has hired your firm without having a pre-existing relationship or already knowing or meeting the professional who will lead or work on the matter (either in person, by video, or by phone). When it happens, it is the exception and usually based upon very strong referrals and reputations.

The fact remains that most new matters/cases/projects (especially complex and/or expensive ones) are awarded to a professional only after in-person, eyeball-to-eyeball contact with the prospective client has been made. Why? Because clients hire lawyers and professionals in whom they have a sense of trust and confidence; those who have credibility and show interest and concern in their problems and have the expertise to help them solve them. These characteristics are not easily assessed or measured based only on information available on the Internet.

The reality is the client development/sales process—like the marketing process—is part art, part science. It is not just what you say or communicate, it's the way you say it, and when that generates results.

Another key to success in client development/sales is understanding the overall process from both the professional's/attorney's *and* the client's perspective.

Over the course of my career, I have created what I refer to as the business development "playing field." It's a step-by-step template of the most common and predictable stages any client or new matter progresses through in order for the attorney/firm to get the new matter in the door. A summarized version appears below:

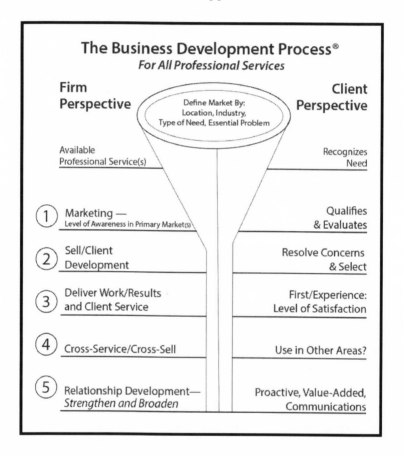

The Business Development Process®
For All Professional Services

Firm Perspective		Client Perspective
	Define Market By: Location, Industry, Type of Need, Essential Problem	
Available Professional Service(s)		Recognizes Need
(1) Marketing — Level of Awareness in Primary Market(s)		Qualifies & Evaluates
(2) Sell/Client Development		Resolve Concerns & Select
(3) Deliver Work/Results and Client Service		First/Experience: Level of Satisfaction
(4) Cross-Service/Cross-Sell		Use in Other Areas?
(5) Relationship Development— *Strengthen and Broaden*		Proactive, Value-Added, Communications

Contrary to what many professionals think and tend to do, once a prospective client contacts you, it is not best to simply "ask for the work" or sale. Rather, the more effective approach is to take a step back once contacted and realize the initial contact is but the first step in a time-honored process that must be applied and finessed for each different situation.

An analogy is the game of football (whether soccer or American football). Those who excel in football have extensive knowledge and understanding of the field, rules, skills, and discipline required to consistently win. Yet, every point or touchdown is scored using a different set of plays. In football, most points are scored using the fundamentals of running, passing, blocking, and tackling in a series over time. Sometimes (but rarely, which is what makes it so exciting), one long kick from the other end of the field ends up in the goal, or one long bomb Hail Mary pass into the end zone produces a touchdown. But these are the exceptions rather than the rule.

The same is true for professional services client development/sales. Most of the business comes in after a series of contacts and communications with the prospective client and other decision makers. Sometimes, but much less often, new business comes in after only one phone call.

In fact, to earn new work, the numerous studies I and others have conducted show that *on average* it takes six to twelve appropriate personal contacts over time to get new business in the door (fewer contacts with a current client and more with potential brand-new clients). This is referred to as a "sales cycle," which is lengthy for most professional services (a "sale" for professional services work can take up to two years or even longer), simply because trust and confidence must be earned, and experience must be obtained. Developing both experience and trust takes time to build.

> Studies show that, on average, it takes 6 to 12 appropriate personal contacts over time to get new business in the door.
>
> – Julie Savarino

Other studies I have conducted over the course of my career (and those by others) show most leads and measurable new work that come from the most commonly used marketing activities (by professionals) (e.g., seminars, speeches, attending trade group conferences, e-alerts, and social media posts) are generated only when combined with a *series* of appropriate personal, one-to-one, direct contacts. For example, calling a potential new client with whom you have no prior relationship or connection nine times in one day will likely not generate new work, but may instead anger and annoy that potential new client and tarnish your reputation.

Consistent, professional, and appropriate outreach and effort over time is what works best to consistently develop new work. As a result, simply attending or speaking at one seminar alone is not enough to develop new clients; more plays must be planned and executed and more time taken to plan to stay in touch and follow-up.

For example, I recently needed to hire and onboard a new, outside professional services provider, one whom I had never worked with before. I obtained referrals from trusted colleagues and reached out. When I spoke to one of them (who came highly recommended), unfortunately, this person did not:

1. Have and use a well-defined new client intake checklist or accompanying process during the initial call with me, nor in subsequent conversations.

2. Search online about me and my company before the initial contact/call.

3. Ask good questions.

4. Show much interest in, not really listen to, or seem to care about my objectives, needs, or deadlines.

5. Ask for the specific information needed to properly scope and price the work.

6. Communicate in a professional, "I am here to serve" manner or tone.

7. Have or use a professional, goodwill-building, efficient, and effective turn-away and refer-out process.

As you can imagine, the above was not an optimal vetting, onboarding, or client experience process and did nothing to enhance the reputation of that outside provider. Those who avoid making these client development/sales mistakes will be more successful at bringing in new business, increasing referrals, and generating positive word-of-mouth.

The key to consistently bringing in new professional services work is to understand the field, rules, skills, and discipline required and to be at the ready to adapt and adjust for each different situation and client. Those without a thorough understanding of how MBDCS flows to bring in new work are operating with a significant handicap. Imagine how effective a football player who did not know the significance of the foul lines on the field would be. Not as effective as those that fully understood their significance to the game.

Most firms still rely primarily on their fee-earners to "sell" the firm's services, while also demanding they bill and collect approximately 1,500 to 1,800 hours of work each year. And too many still use a hit-or-miss, opportunistic, "random acts of lunch" approach to marketing and client development, because they lack a full and complete understanding of the entire business development process as described in this chapter.

How does this hit-or-miss, opportunistic approach play out? Often, they may utilize one marketing tool, such as a seminar, which may or may not generate personal contacts. Then they will say, "Marketing doesn't work." Alternately, when professionals actually do make a personal contact, they do not necessarily recognize it as a client development opportunity and have no system or procedure of approach and follow-up. Again, they will say, "Marketing doesn't work." But, this conclusion rests upon a lack of knowledge and understanding of how MBDCS works to generate new professional services business.

The missing link in many firms is a formal and proactive client-development/sales process and program to support and drive the most profitable, organic growth (see Chapter 10 for more information about organic growth strategies and tactics). The fact is, without an organized client development/sales program that includes well-planned and coordinated direct, personal, or face-to-face communication with clients, prospects, and referral sources, the chances of converting marketing efforts into qualified leads (conversion rate) and generating measurable new business as a result are not great.

The ideal goal of every single penny of a firm's or practitioner's marketing investment is (or should be) to generate qualified leads. A qualified lead is when an existing client, target prospective client, or referral source communicates a question or an interest in a certain issue, problem, or topic. Most often, qualified leads come in the form of questions a client or prospective client asks, such as, "Does your firm have a written cybersecurity policy it recommends?" or "Does your firm do FCPA work?" or "Are any of your partners experienced in oil and gas?" etc. Clients or prospects ask these kinds of questions because they have (or someone they know has) a need for counsel, advice, or representation.

Once a need is identified, it needs to be qualified, i.e., it needs to meet the criteria of being a "qualified lead."[41] Qualification consists of an internal review or assessment of the lead, which answers these (and other) questions in the affirmative: "Are there any conflicts?" "Is this the type of client our firm wants?" "Is this the type of legal work our firm wants and does well?", and other qualification criteria unique to the firm, type of work, and ideal client.

Then, the only way any qualified lead is converted into new work (conversion rate) for the firm is if someone in the firm communicates directly with the person(s) who expressed the need. A firm partner (or another firm representative) needs to get in touch, stay in touch, respond appropriately and in a timely manner, follow up, and follow through to develop the lead and relationship into new work or a new client. Lead qualification and relationship development are jobs and responsibilities that, in the past, have been traditionally handled by firm lawyers, but this is changing due to the time, effort, skill, and discipline these processes take. (See Chapter 10 for examples of what some firms are doing.)

What are the main criteria that all clients use to find, vet and hire outside professional services providers?

1. Expertise – Answers the question: Do you do *this*? How highly are you recommended? And by whom?

2. Experience – Answers this question: How many times have you done this and to what result? What is your reputation?

3. Conflicts – Is there a current legal and/or business conflict? Potential?

4. Business Goals – Do you align with our definition of success? Our needs in areas of geography, level of risk for this matter, budget/cost expectations, working relationship.

5. Matter Management – Case/matter strategy? Options? Staffing? Diversity? Use of metrics?

6. Service Features – Level of flexibility and listening to understand? Responsiveness? Status Reporting? Invoicing and billing options? Use of technology?

7. Cost Sensitivity/Effectiveness – Use of leverage? What could be done in-house or outsourced? Discounts and/or alternative billing?

8. Personal Fit – Chemistry, Empathy; How do you interact? Do we like each other?

Studies I have conducted over the course of my career show that number 8 above, personal fit, often has the greatest impact on the selection.

Your Client's Perspective

At all times, the goal of every client is to find and hire the best lawyer or other professional for the matter, case, engagement, or project at hand. Clients seek to match the result they want with the professional or firm that most closely aligns with what they want and need done. All clients seek to finish and conclude their work in the best and most cost-effective manner possible. Ultimately, all clients want solutions to their problems delivered in a timely, efficient, and cost-effective manner.

> Your clients are not yours alone! You are competing and being evaluated every day on every project, matter, or engagement.
>
> – Julie Savarino

All clients place value on client service, efficient work, industry knowledge, knowledge of the client's business, the firm's people, organizational structure, philosophy, and culture, each of which varies in emphasis depending upon the client, problem, situation, matter, or case.

All clients are risk-averse when they procure outside professional services, even more so during economic crises. As a result, they give more weight to past successful experiences (their own or by referral from trusted colleagues) as the best predictor of future performance, upon which they rely to minimize the risk of suboptimal performance and results. So, experience and track record are the primary criteria clients use to develop a short list of providers or firms from which they will make their ultimate selection.

Most often, clients' short lists reside in their minds only, but short lists are increasingly being formalized into writing, so a request for proposal/qualifications (RFP) can be sent. The use of RFPs to procure outside professional services via a formal competitive bidding process is required by law for some organizations, but many other clients are now opting to use automated RFPs because they often result in the client saving significant fees and costs.

Examples of some modern technologies being used that automate the RFP process include RFP360, https://rfp360.com/, PERSUIT, (www.persuit.com), BanyanRFP (www.banyanrfp.com), and others. Given time limits, most outside practitioners quickly cobble together responses to these automated RFPs, not realizing there are skills required to optimize their response when competing for work using modern automated RFPs or reverse auctions. Also, in many firms, RFP responses are not tracked, coordinated or reported on in a metric and data-driven manner.

The use of modern and proven technology to optimize all MBDCS investments has never been greater. Jason Noble, a technology expert, who serves as President and CEO of Ikaun, (www.ikaun.com) says, "The need to develop new business efficiently has never been greater. Modern technologies allow firms to automatically aggregate various sources of relevant business development data and information. Adopting them improves the ROI from the firm's business development spend because they allow the in-house marketing team to increase the accuracy, timeliness, and quality of deliverables. The use of these types of technologies is a must in order to continue to increase productivity and profitability."

Here is a list of the approximate return on investment (ROI) from commonly used MBDCS tools:

Approximate/Relative* ROI from Common Business Development Tools Used by Professional Services Firms & Providers

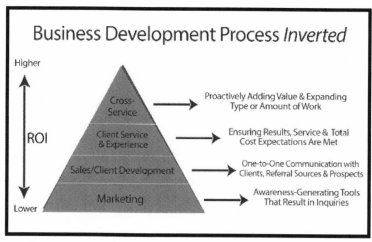

Highest ROI: Client Service & Relationship Development Tools

- Complimentary, Annual Client Reviews — on satisfaction, service, needs, etc.
- One-to-One or Small Group Meetings – in a private and secure setting
- Client Visits, Plant, Facilities and/or Office Tours
- Work a Day a Week at Client's Office/For the Client Only and Secondments
- Private, Secure and Robust Intranets for Clients and Other Tailored Technology Options

- Tailored Seminars, Webinars, Client Events — at client's office, with formal continuing education credits
- Tailored, Invitation-Only Education Programs for Select Prospects or Referral Sources
- Proprietary Research — sharing and publishing results of surveys/studies
- Blogs and Email Newsletters – specifically defined to precise markets, types of businesses, industry, problem or area
- Firm Alumni Programs
- Social Media – LinkedIn and Twitter
- Community/Charitable Events and Partnerships With Clients

Critical firm/internal MBDCS systems, processes, procedures & relevant support staff

- Fully Populated, Staffed, Maintained and Used CRM/Enterprise Relationship Database – including client-facing market definitions
- Formalized Firmwide Service Process and Deliverables — touchpoints and value optimized from cradle to grave and beyond
- Formal Client Service Teams – including a dedicated support staff and reporting function
- Individual Business Development Plans – required by firm management, tracked, reviewed and tied to compensation
- Individual Business Development Budget Allocations — tied to plans, including accompanying support, review and approval processes
- Defined, Organized and Disciplined Client Development/Sales Pipelines and Processes – tied to individual business plans, budgets, and a dedicated staff support and reporting function
- Initiated Proposals – not reacting to an RFP/I/Q, instead proactively sending to a qualified lead
- Responding to RFP/Q/Is — strategic, selective, organized and professional

Necessary Marketing & Positioning Tools
- Web Presence – a search engine optimized (SEO) website
- Attorney Biographical Sketches – including up-to-date photos, representative matters, and video clips
- Public Speaking — for those who are great speakers, public speaking is often a high ROI
- Trade Show Sponsorship
- Board Involvement and Leadership Positions: Business and Non-Profit Boards
- Involvement In and Attending Industry/Trade/Charitable/Civic Group Meetings – but for some, this is a high ROI
- Publishing on Amazon, Google books, etc.
- By-Lined Articles and Getting Quoted in Major Media
- Alliances and Networks
- Club Memberships – social, sporting and special interest clubs
- Select Community Relations and Charitable Support

Lower ROI: Broadcast-Level Marketing & Communications Tools
- Sky Boxes
- Media Mentions/Public Relations
- Generic, Firm-Sponsored Events, Office Opening and Receptions
- Brochures and Practice Group Descriptions
- Firm-Centric Newsletters and Alerts
- Advertising – Television, Radio, Print

*The above is not exhaustive of every possible tool/communication/ outreach, nor do the above levels of ROI apply precisely to any individual firm or practice, because the MBDCS tools that generate the best ROI for any given firm or practice vary based on a number of factors.

An excellent MBDCS effort was done by Morrison & Foerster (www.mofo.com) in March 2020. The firm conducted a survey of in-house legal professionals, asking about the impacts the crisis was having on their business. The results of the survey were shared with the firm's key clients/contacts and also widely-published and quoted in April 2020. This type of survey is known as proprietary research and is a proven MBDCS tool that has been used for decades by many leading professional services firms, such as the Big Four accounting firms, major consulting firms like Bain and McKinsey, and others.

Why is proprietary research an excellent MBDCS tool? Because one-of-a-kind research provides the firm and its practitioners new insights into their target markets and client base, adds meaningful information to clients and prospects through tailored educational programs and consultations, and the results from well done surveys often get a lot of publicity, which extends the firm's market position and brand.

As Jeff Bezos, founder of Amazon said years ago, "I very frequently get the question: 'What's going to change in the next 10 years?' And that is a very interesting question; it's a very common one. I almost never get the question: *'What's not going to change in the next 10 years?'* And I submit to you that that second question is actually the more important of the two—because you can build a business strategy around the things that are stable in time."[42]

What will *not change* is clients' needs and desires to obtain cost-effective solutions to their problems. Yet, due to the pandemic's requiring social distancing, all MBDCS tools need to be reevaluated. Client-centric, value-added, solutions-oriented tools and communications will still yield the best ROI, but most will need to be delivered virtually.

The most profitable and successful firms know that marketing and client development/sales tools and efforts gets the work and clients in the door, but the key to long-term success is the *level of client service* delivered firmwide.

The importance of consistently excellent client service

Even if your firm markets itself very well and has a well-honed marketing and client development/sales process in place, it is still not enough to build an excellent reputation and new-business generation "machine." What is required, once the matter is won (i.e., business is brought in the door), is to effectively service the matter, which requires a combination of results and delivery tools. The client service process is also somewhat predictable, linear, and systematic.

Numerous studies conducted by many leading businesses, including American Express,[43] and from over twenty years of studies conducted by BTI Consulting Group (www.bticonsulting.com), show that the firms with the best client service are the most profitable, have the best reputations and brand recognition, and attract the best talent, clients, and opportunities. So, excellent client service is the number-one differentiator, yet too few firms or practitioners have optimal systems, processes, and procedures in place to ensure excellent service at scale.

> Excellent client service (from the client's perspective) is the main differentiator of all professional services.
>
> – Julie Savarino

Exceptional client service requires more than great lawyers and fee-earners alone. Clients' expectations can only be met today by the combination of 1) the technical acumen of the lawyers; 2) the operational and strategic expertise and insight of other business professionals; along with 3) the use of modern technologies.[44]

An example of how business professionals can add value to firms comes from a major buyer of outside legal and other professional services, Cammie Teems, Risk Manager for Bestway USA (www.bestwaycorp.us), who says, "We sent a formal RFP to various law firms. Only one firm offered a dedicated client service professional as part of its proposal, a position that I had never heard of before. She added considerable value to our interview, selection, and onboarding processes, and is of tremendous assistance." (full disclosure: the client service professional she mentions is the author).

In order to deliver excellent client service (from the client's perspective), it is critical to know what clients want, desire, and expect from the beginning, so your service and deliverables can align with those expectations as much as possible. The fact is client expectations are set early on in any relationship or new engagement with their professional services provider(s) and firms. Ask yourself:

- How good are you at setting and managing client expectations?

- How proactive are you at providing clients with predictability and transparency before a matter, engagement, or case even begins?

- How good are your intake habits and routine? (see Chapter 8 for more information on habits.)

Take the client intake process, for example. The steps, approach, and steps used each time varies by fee-earner and also within the same firm. Most professionals use their own, often haphazard intake process to onboard new clients (after completing any required "New Client/Matter Intake" forms and procedures).

To enhance your onboarding process, consider creating and using a checklist (ideally automated) of other client-centric information to gather questions to ask your clients, as appropriate, over time. Such as researching (or requesting research be conducted) on the below or asking these relevant questions, ideally early in the relationship:

- ✓ What are the client's key markets, and what is happening in that/those markets?

- ✓ What is the company's or organization's current financial status, and what are the trends?

✓ What is the company's long-term strategy and vision? What is their end game/exit plan?

✓ What types of needs does the company have?

✓ What are the primary personal goals and concerns of the key decision-makers?

✓ What is most important to the people whom you/the firm will be working with most during the engagement?

✓ What are the personality and communication styles of the decision-makers?

✓ What is the client's expectation and budget/expected total cost of this case/matter/engagement?

✓ Are there any special billing or partnering arrangements they would like or would be interested in?

✓ How satisfied are they with the service and quality of the fee earners and staff at your firm with whom they work?

✓ What does the client know about other services and solutions the firm could provide?

Some of this information can be obtained from publicly available sources; some through networking with accountants, underwriters, bankers, etc.; some can come from people at your firm who know people in the client's organization, etc. The best way to get this information, however, is by communicating directly with key people to learn their needs, goals and styles.

See Chapter 10 for more suggestions on ways to upgrade your client intake process.

So, what are some other best business development practices in an era of social distancing? Remember what is important: not where you meet, but the quality and content of the communication.

▪ Just because you cannot go to lunch does not mean you cannot have meaningful conversations with clients, contacts, and prospective clients.

- Make efforts to be indispensable to key clients. How? Schedule time to monitor their industry and organization, and conduct research relating to them/their needs; consider "what-if" scenarios; identify information that could be of use or value to them; and schedule and initiate regular proactive outreach.
- List all the socially distant ways and means you have to communicate, such as telephone, email, video-conferencing apps, webinar apps, secure messaging apps, LinkedIn and other social media messaging and events, fax, snail mail, drop-offs, or, when allowed, physically in-person meetings.
  - Identify the ones you are not using but that your clients/contact use and consider signing up or obtaining them.
  - Make time to learn how to use new ones, and to optimize your use of new technology.
- All communications should lead with empathy, by asking how they are doing personally, by suspending all judgment and assumptions about their situation, and by preparing to deliver relevant and useable information in the format they prefer.
- When writing:
  - Remember that the subject line and first few sentences are the most important to grab the reader's attention.
  - Provide context and a road map by answering the "Five Ws and H": Who, What, When, Where, Why, and How, using about forty words or less.
  - Use examples when possible.
  - Highlight or mark conclusions, options, need to dos, or action items.
  - Create and use custom images as appropriate and when possible, such as infographics, flowcharts, checklists, etc.
- When using video conferencing or webinar apps:
  - Test your Internet speed and optimize for video.
  - Know which apps your clients use and create an account for each.
  - Customize your background/back-drop.
  - Optimize the lighting surrounding you.

o   Create the capability to silence all background noise.

o   Square your head to the camera, and test view yourself to adjust.

o   Pace your speech a bit slower when communicating online to account for lags and bandwidth delays.

o   When clients or contacts agree to speak on a webinar your firm is producing, offer to make an appropriate donation to their favorite charity or pro bono effort in their name.

- When possible and as appropriate, consider drop-offs. A drop-off can be appropriate for clients and contacts who live or work near you. Examples include purchasing sealed food or beverages, or other sanitary items for clients, contacts, and/or their family.

- When possible and as appropriate, ask clients and contacts whether they would like to meet for coffee or a meal, preferably outside, like at a park or a coffee shop that has large-scale outdoor seating. Wear a face mask and keep a 6 to 15-foot distance from them at all times.

There is so much more information, nuance, and detail associated with effective MBDCS for professional services that I need to write another book on that topic alone. In the meantime, some additional information and resources can be found in later chapters of this book and in the appendixes.

Key Takeaways

- ➢ Business development is the most important function for any professional services practice to even exist, not to mention to survive and thrive.

- ➢ Consistently developing new business for a professional services firm or practice is part art, part science.

- ➢ To optimize results from MBDCS investments and activities, they must be carefully selected, thoroughly implemented, and followed up upon. MBDCS is a bona fide business discipline that takes investments and efforts over time to generate consistent results.

➢ Embrace the fact that you are your brand. Everyone who works at your firm is a brand ambassador who adds to or detracts from your firm's reputation and image with every action, every deliverable, and every communication.

➢ Business development is a business discipline and an overall process, touching every aspect of the practice, and is further defined by 1) marketing, 2) client development/sales, 3) client service, and 4) cross-service (MBDCS).

➢ Know and embrace the science (body of knowledge) about what MBDCS works and what does not for professional services firms.

➢ Developing new business is not simply common sense, luck, or a "soft skill" that someone either has or does not have.

➢ During or after the pandemic, make the time to review, analyze and rank all your business development investments and efforts, including all MBDCS activities for ROI, client value, necessity, and efficacy.

➢ It is not possible to measure the ROI of every single MBDCS program or effort.

➢ Work to improve ROI from MBDCS by utilizing greater discipline in your current investments and practices.

➢ Consider the best investments in people, process, and technologies to build your practice now and in the future, the balance of which varies from firm to firm depending on type of practice, strategic plans, and many other factors.

8

OBJECTIVELY ASSESS YOUR HABITS, ROUTINES, & USE OF PROCESS

All successful professional services providers are busy. Pandemics cause numerous distractions and even greater demands on available time. Yet, each of us has the same twenty-four hours in each day.

As discussed in Chapter 6, analyzing your use of time is critical. It is important for all busy professionals to schedule time in their calendar to do what is important but not necessarily urgent. Given time demands and the realities of life and work, unless you **make yourself** formally schedule time and auto-reminders to do work that is important but non-urgent, the chances you will ever attend to it or get it done is small. As a result, the level of your future success could be diminished.

To be productive, most professionals already have a variety of practice-related habits and routines in place, which vary from person to person. Habits and routines are proven to drive productivity and results.

Yet, many professionals have common habits and routines that inhibit optimal productivity, performance, and results, which are usually caused by weak time management and personal discipline. What are the most common habits that are not necessarily productive in the long run?

- Reacting to your cell, mobile, or office telephone every time it rings or receives a notification.

- Allowing any distraction to take your focus away from your work or waylay your best intentions.

- Using antiquated, manual, and time-intensive ways of completing a task or project.

- Not scheduling or taking the time to learn about, get trained on, and adopt proven technologies.

If you have never or not recently taken the time to assess your time management skills and the associated techniques you use for work, now is the time to do so. There are many ways to do so described in this book, along with many other available resources.

This chapter is designed to highlight some common habits and routines related to marketing, business development, communications, and client service (MBDCS), which, if upgraded, adapted or changed could help increase your future success.

Habit: Using (or not using) your firm's CRM (customer/client relationship management) system

We are all in the people business, and there is only one (or a very few) place/s where all relevant professional contacts are maintained in a useable format: either in the firm's CRM system, in an individual practitioner's Outlook contacts/other contact management systems, and/or on LinkedIn.

If you do not have an accessible list of all contacts in writing, then the only contacts you'll keep in touch with are the ones the you happen to think of, which means many fall by the wayside or are forgotten about. This fuels a highly reactive practice that misses many opportunities. For example, once done with a case or engagement, most practitioners simply move on to the next client, the next project or matter, without being sure to capture all relevant information about the client or referral sources they just finished working for. Not tangibly capturing all people and contacts is a mistake that narrows your pool of potential opportunities.

Most professional services firms with twenty-five or more fee-earners have an automated, somewhat centralized CRM (customer/client relationship management) system, such as Intapp's OnePlace for Marketing (www.intapp.com), DealCloud (https://dealcloud.com), SalesForce (www.salesforce.com), or ContactEase, (http://colevalley.com). A CRM system is one technology platform that contains all the firm's clients and other contacts, as aggregated from Outlook and other contact management platforms.

But, most CRM systems in firms are not being used to their full potential, because they are not complete or fully populated. Why? Because every or any partner/owner can and does "opt-out" fully or partially, i.e., chooses not to include all their clients and contacts, or chooses not to add any individual client or contact into the CRM system. Many professionals "opt-out" due to a desire to protect their client information.

Those professionals who do not regularly use their firm's CRM system are missing out on its power to help build their practice. Just think about the power of people. The average professional services provider knows approximately 250 people and has the same number of contacts. A firm with twenty partners then has approximately 5,000 contacts, and "who you know" is power. Having all firm contacts accessible in one place/CRM system can create new opportunities and greatly enhance existing opportunities for new business.

For example, a partner had always wanted to work with and for a certain company but did not know anyone who worked there. When the CRM system was checked, it turned out that two of his partners knew people who did. One partner's neighbor was the CFO, and another partner went to college with another C-suite executive of the company. Having this information allowed the client development team to work with the partners to craft an appropriate series of outreaches, which ultimately (approximately a year and a half later, after a series of relevant communications and follow-up) led to an initial work assignment from the company. After completing the initial assignment successfully, the partner and firm were asked to propose for the entire line of work, which they won. Now, that client is one of the firm's largest.

Another example illustrates how to use the CRM system to avoid missteps or embarrassment to you and your firm. A firm lawyer wanted to meet with a friend who worked in compliance at a global manufacturing company. Before arranging the meeting, he checked the firm's CRM system. Unbeknownst to him at the time, it did not produce any hits because the lawyers who knew people in that company had not added them into the firm's CRM system and the firm's CRM system was not automated to flag for potential conflicts.

So, he set up and held the meeting, which led to significant embarrassment to and for the firm because many other partners in the firm knew others who worked for the company (who called them) and the firm was currently handling a dispute adverse to the company. This is the type of relationship faux pas that should be avoided at all costs, yet this type of overlapping, non-coordinated and ultimately embarrassing to the firm outreach occurs often due to a lack of firmwide and utilized process, procedure, and/or modern technology.

Let's look at some other MBDCS routines and habits you can review or consider incorporating into your practice and schedule.

Habit: Your mindset, thinking, and knowledge about effective MBDCS

Below are some key questions to ask yourself regarding your current MBDCS mindset and thinking habits. Consider which you are weakest on, and which—if you made changes or upgrades—would help you thrive and be even more successful.

Do You Intentionally and Consciously Know and Embrace the Following Thinking?

1. Sitting, waiting, and hoping for clients and work to come to you no longer works in today's highly competitive market.
2. MBDCS is a discipline that needs to be paid attention to, worked on, and applied consistently over time. It is not a one-off, point-in-time transaction.

3. What works to develop business over the course of a career is consistent, strategic focus and efforts over time.
4. Clients, colleagues, and all other people are the most valuable asset of your profession and practice.
5. Are you committed to:
    a. Treating, interacting, and communicating with all people in a professional and respectful manner?
    b. Getting the best possible results for client?
    c. Providing excellent, responsive, and proactive and initiated client service?
    d. Nurturing client relationships by staying in touch on a regular basis, seeking feedback, celebrating clients' successes, and showing appreciation for a client's business and friendship?
    e. Conducting end-of-matter or periodic client satisfaction/feedback discussions, and using the information gained to upgrade and improve?
6. Clients usually hire professional services providers because of a natural outgrowth of an authentic relationship, one based on trust and confidence, which needs to be continually reinforced.

Is this your Intentional, Conscious Commitment to MBDCS?

1. You regularly and strategically invest in yourself and your career success.
2. MBDCS is a priority to you.
3. You devote approximately 200-400 hours a year to MBDCS annually, and you track your time/efforts accordingly.
    - At a minimum, you invest 200 hours annually on MBDCS, of which 70% (or 210 hours) are direct one-to-one or small group meeting/conversations, and approximately 30% (or 90 hours) is invested in speaking, writing, blogging, posting on social media, and other broadcasting activities.

4. You make and take time for MBDCS regularly and consistently.

5. In all MBDCS efforts and activities, always use and follow the 5 Ps: Prior Preparation Prevents Poor Performance.

6. You undertake MBDCS planning and activities with the same level of commitment, effort, and focus that you devote to serving your clients.

7. You avoid "random acts of lunch" and instead prepare and implement good questions to ask, issues to raise, and/or "by the way" comments for each (see "Proactively Asking Great Questions" below).

8. You use and mark your automated calendar to follow-up and stay in touch.

Are These Your Conscious Expectations Around Getting Results from MBDCS?

1. MBDCS requires patience, persistence, and follow-up, because few MBDCS activities produce immediate results.

2. MBDCS-related studies, research and statistics show that:

   - Only 3-4% of professional services providers are "natural" rainmakers. The rest of us must make a conscious and deliberate effort over time to become better at developing new business.

   - It takes–on average–nine appropriate contacts or communications over time to earn new legal work.

   - The time it takes to meet a new potential client and then get some of their work can be anywhere from three months to ten years or more! The average time is approximately two years.

   - Less than three percent of all new work is won on the first attempt at communication. It is very unlikely that going to one lunch with a prospect will result in a hiring decision on the spot (although it does happen very rarely).

- Most people hire a lawyer or other professional services provider only when they have a need for their services–for example, when a problem arises that no one internally knows how to resolve or has the bandwidth to address; they have been sued, when something happens that requires legal or other professional advice, when a deal or transaction arises, etc.
- People like and tend to hire those with similar personal styles to their own. Or, appreciate, value, and hire those with opposite or different styles/attributes.

Habit: Winging many MBDCS efforts

An old adage from the military says in essence, "Lack of prior preparation leads to poor performance." Most professional services providers would never dream of not preparing before a negation, board meeting, court appearance, or any other meeting or communication needed to deliver top-quality service and results to a client.

Yet, due to intense time pressures and other factors, many professional services providers either fail to take time to prepare or simply "wing it" when implementing many common MBDCS activities. For example, while many lawyers are great orators in a courtroom, not all are great public speakers. Presenting before a jury or judge is much different than making a speech to an industry or trade show audience, at a continuing legal education (CLE) event, or presenting to other groups of people.

The same holds true for new-client meetings. Also due to time pressures, many professionals do not take the time to prepare for or to create an organized system and routine to prepare for new client meetings. As a result, there is no consistency in terms of the questions asked or information gathered and shared with the prospective new client. For tips on how to upgrade new client meetings and intake processes, see Chapter 10.

Habit: Not having an organizational system and routine for MBDCS

Many professionals do not have or use:

- A strategic MBDCS list, such as a top client/referral source past client outreach list that they refer to, use to proactively stay in touch, and upgrade. Now is the time to create one.

- An organized filing system by client, project, type, or message.

- A system or habit of adding MBDCS efforts into their weekly planning time and to-do list.

- A routine for every person you meet, everyone on each case/matter, and every business card obtained. Most professionals do not:

    1) create an Outlook contact for each of them

    2) connect with them on LinkedIn

    3) send them relevant firm "opt-in" lists for emails/blogs, and/or

    4) have them added to the firm's CRM system.

- Never-ending, weekly, auto-recurring Outlook/calendar meetings with themselves as follow-up and stay in touch reminders.

- LinkedIn before traveling. Checking your connections who live in an area you will be traveling to can help make the best use of time and stay in touch with key contacts during trips.

- Technology to stay abreast of clients, industries, new developments, etc.

Habit: Not optimally using available assistance and not asking for assistance

Most professional services providers already have a trusted professional assistant. Some do not have a fully dedicated professional assistant, but instead share that person's time with other fee-earners. Regardless, it is essential to have great support staff to help get work done and leverage your limited available time for MBDCS, yet many professionals fail to use their assistants optimally.

Meet with your assistant, and explain your MBDCS goals, objectives, and strategic initiatives. Ask then whether they have the bandwidth to assist you, and if so, how. For example, you could ask your assistant to take all telephone calls for you during certain hours of each day so you can remain focused and undistracted (except for emergencies, of course).

Most professional services firms also have dedicated, internal MBDCS support staff. Consider meeting with them to ask what services and tools they might be able to provide to assist you with MBDCS. Same with your firm's librarians and information technology staff. They, too, may have tools or ways they could help you make the best use of your MBDCS time and efforts.

There are other ways to leverage and make the best use of your MBDCS time and efforts. You could consider outsourcing by vetting and hire a proven client development/sales coach, content producer, or virtual assistant.

Habit: Not investing in or making time to upgrade your knowledge and skills

Regularly engaging in professional development has been proven to help drive success. Yet many professionals do not have either the time or interest in improving their practices or habits.

Some professional development is required in most firms, such as obtaining necessary CE (continuing education) credits to maintain licensure; sexual harassment, diversity, crisis readiness, new technology, or unconscious bias training sessions (to name a few).

But most practitioners can use more and different professional development, which varies from professional to professional. One way to identify what professional development would be best to increase your future success is to read this guidebook and mark the items you are most interested in improving, then seek ways to efficiently get the information, knowledge or skills you need. More information on knowledge is in Chapter 7 of this book.

Habit: Making choices based mainly on what is most convenient for you

Remember that the client's perspective and preferences are what matter most. So, suggest meetings in ways that would be most convenient to the client. For example, do not ask them to meet you at your office, unless it is necessary to do so. Ask them whether they would prefer a videoconference instead of their having to take time out of their schedule to travel to and from your office. Avoid calling in-person meetings when a secure email or message would suffice.

Habit: Proactively asking great, strategic questions

The easiest and least time-consuming way to consistently generate new opportunities and secure client relationships is to start asking strategic questions or changing the conversation. Or better yet, getting into the habit of regularly asking clients and contacts new or different questions.

I guarantee that doing so will double or triple the number of qualified opportunities you learn about/spot and can double, triple, or even quadruple your book of business. How to do this? By making an effort to incorporate the "add-on" or "by the way" ask or statements into your routine. What is an add-on or by-the-way ask or statement?

A by-the-way question or statement can be initiated when you are wrapping up a one-to-one client status update telephone call, when you are leaving a client meeting, or when walking out of a restaurant (or somewhere else where you cannot be overheard). You ask the client or contact an additional question such as:

By the way...

- How is COMPANY/ENTITY NAME handling X (such as data security or breach protection)?

- Saw in the news that COMPANY/ENTITY is expanding into X. I would love to hear about it.

- I saw on LinkedIn that you know X. Let me know if I could go to lunch with you two. I would love to meet him/her.

- Anything new or developing over at COMPANY/ENTITY?

- How is/are the X project/plans progressing?

- Is there anything my firm or I can be doing to better serve you/COMPANY/ENTITY?

- Thank you for referring [NAME] to me. I would very much appreciate your mentioning my name to others who may need legal advice or representation.

Here are some examples of add-on phrases, questions and statements:

Before we hang up...

- I wanted to ask how the X project is going.

- I read that a new general counsel started a few weeks ago. Do you think I could meet him/her at some point? If so, what do you suggest?

- I wanted to ask whether your company/firm would be interested in any continuing education topics that members of my firm could present at your office for you and your colleagues at a mutually convenient time.

- I wanted to ask you a favor, please. I saw on LinkedIn that you are connected to _____. Would you be willing to introduce me to him/her? If so, I would be happy to treat you both to lunch or coffee at your convenience.

I would not be doing my job if...

- I did not ask about/raise the issue of your corporate compliance program. Since the company has faced X lawsuits this year, it may be a good use of time for us to discuss and review COMPANY'S/ENTITY'S compliance program sometime soon.

- I did not let you know that my law firm offers a full range of services. Because you work in wealth management, it would likely be beneficial for you to meet my partner [NAME]. Would you like me to set up a meeting?

From time to time ...

- I like to take a step back with my existing clients like you and ask _____.

- I like to remind all my existing referral sources like you that not only can you refer _____ cases to me, but you can consider referring _____ also.

Asking new or different questions using the by-the-way or add-on techniques described above works not just with existing clients and contacts. Consider doing the same whenever you meet someone new. Be curious and, when attending a seminar, event, or conference, try asking, "Are you enjoying this event/conference?"

The key to short- and long-term success is to work on making *asking* new or different questions a *habit*, something you do regularly without even thinking about it with all people, clients, and contacts in your life. Remember that creating a new habit takes approximately sixty to ninety days of consistent implementation and practice before it becomes second-nature. So, to remind yourself, consider adding "ask other questions" to your to-do list or schedule; adding new or different questions to ask on your business development plan; and/or write the word "ask" on a sticky note and attach it to your computer screen. See Chapter 6, and Appendixes 2 and 3 for more information.

To bring in new business, it is usually not enough to simply ask new or better questions. You must capture the contacts and information gained and follow up on it (not just in your head, but put it in *writing*). When I worked as a professional business developer for a major accounting firm, the firm's mantra was "convert conversations into writing" and "get proposals out," both of which are proven techniques to create and maintain a pipeline of new opportunities.

If you need help converting a conversation into writing, ask a member of your firm's marketing or business development team or a qualified outside coach to assist you in drafting appropriate emails, service offerings, call scripts, and other strategic communications, as appropriate.

The Science of Habits

If you want to enhance, improve, and/or develop new or better MBDCS-related habits, you must make a commitment to yourself to do so. Remember: being committed to something means you will get it done no matter what distraction may arise.

It is one thing to create a new habit and another to make it automatic, both of which take a commitment and considerable effort over time. According to a study published in the *European Journal of Social Psychology*, it takes 18 to 254 days—or, on average, 136 days or 44 months—for a person to form a new habit,. This study also concluded that, on average, it takes 66 days—or more than two months—for a new behavior to become automatic. How long it takes a new habit to form can vary widely depending on the behavior, the person, and the circumstances.

Below are eight best practices to upgrade an existing or create a new habit:

1. **Know and embrace the proven fact that habits and routines are hard to change.** Existing habits and routines will not change by thinking about them for a minute, ten minutes, a half-hour, or a day; nor will they change by wanting, wishing, and/or hoping they change. It takes conscious, methodical effort over time to change habits or embed new habits into your routine as described below.

2. **Realize, accept, and embrace the fact that 90% of effective business development starts and lives in your mind.** In your mind lies your level of personal self-discipline, your self-control over your use of time, and your self-control and choices in response to external cues and situations and how you handle/respond to distractions. Much of effective business

development consists of self-discipline, acting, and committing sweat/effort, even when you do not want to or do not feel like it.

3. **First, you must commit.** If you are only somewhat interested in changing a habit or embedding a new, upgraded habit into your routine, studies show you will likely not accomplish it. You must *commit*. The difference between interest and commitment is intensity of will–which lies in your mind. If you are committed, you will do whatever it takes; no hurdle/distraction will stand in your way, you will make it happen, and you will do it. On the other hand, if you are mildly interested, you may do it when you think of it or have extra time, but because you are really not 100% committed, you will likely blow it off for various reasons. So, commit!

4. **Plan ahead.** Multiple studies show that the more thoughtfully and thoroughly you plan, the greater are your chances of success. Other studies show that reducing a plan to writing more than doubles your chance of success. A lengthy plan is not necessary; a simple list and/or recurring auto-reminders in Outlook about what you want to do and when will suffice. Periodically, at least once a year, you should review your plan and progress against your original goals and objectives and adjust accordingly.

5. **Know and impress *reasonable expectations* in your mind.** To embed any new habit into your routine such that it becomes second nature–something you automatically do without much extra effort–multiple studies show that it takes (on average) sixty to ninety days of consistent, conscious effort. Know this ahead of time, and plan for it.

6. **Create and use external and/or visual cues.** Have a list in writing. Program your mobile device(s)/Outlook to auto-remind you and use Outlook categories. Put a "sticky note" note on your

phone. Do whatever works for you to visually remind you/cue you about your commitment.

7. **Plan ahead for challenges, hurdles, distractions, and weak motivation, and have a plan in place to handle them.** For example, every Thursday after lunch close your office door and ask your assistant to hold all calls for half an hour while you review and get in touch with clients, referral sources and/or contacts. If you are interrupted or distracted, discipline yourself to complete the efforts/tasks another time and mark it in your schedule.

8. **Realize, accept and embrace that *repetition is the force of habit*.** Hundreds of studies prove this. So, build into your plan, for a period of at least ninety days, a cadence of repetition that works for you. For example, if you want to become a huge rainmaker, build at least fifteen to thirty minutes of business development time into each day. Or discipline yourself to review and stay in touch with select contacts as appropriate every Thursday after lunch, for example.

Habit: Your use of process(es) – beyond what is described above.

This topic, along with process mapping, is covered in detail in Chapter 10 of this book.

Key Takeaways

> ➤ Embrace the discipline needed to be successful and the power of habits.
> ➤ Adopt an authentic willingness to invest in yourself and others.
> ➤ Enhance the way you habitually think about and define MBDCS (see Chapter 7).
> ➤ Schedule time to prepare for MBDCS efforts (see Chapter 6).

- ➤ Create an organizational system and routine for MBDCS.
- ➤ Enlist support and ask for assistance for your MBDCS efforts and related work.
- ➤ Invest in and make time to upgrade relevant MBDCS knowledge and skills.
- ➤ Schedule communications based on what will be most convenient for your client/contact.
- ➤ Proactively ask great, strategic questions and add-on ask statements.

9

OBJECTIVELY AND STRATEGICALLY ASSESS YOUR PRACTICE, COMPETITIVE POSITION & SITUATION

Know that time is of the essence. In a pandemic, change occurs at lightning speed and does not slow down. The cascading effect of numerous dominos falling often simultaneously and continually within many parts of the economy, means the need for speed has never been greater.

Expense ledger, cost control, and optimization

In the wake of the 2020 pandemic, most clients of all professional services firms and providers (except for the relatively few clients whose demand has remained stable or has exploded) were directed by clients to eliminate, reduce, and control all non-essential, non-mission-critical costs and expenses immediately and in a measurable and meaningful manner.

Many clients took dramatic steps to do so, such as:
- Putting stop-orders on engagements and projects
- Demanding decreased hourly rates
- Demanding caps or not-to-exceed limits on existing work
- Settling open cases and closing open matters
- Decreasing the number of outside professional services firms and providers they use

Internally within professional services firms, these same demands were made to every practice group and every administrative support department. Firm leaders asked all practice and administrative departments to reassess their budgets and planned hiring and spend and to make cuts in a measurable and meaningful manner.

Controlling firm and practice-related expenses and costs is very important during both good times and bad. But be aware, in the wake of a crisis, the natural human, knee-jerk, instinctive reaction is to cut costs to the bone. While cost-control is critical, going overboard on cost cutting without a careful, holistic, and strategic review and consideration can threaten your future survival.

One way to analyze your expenses is to consider your highest cost centers. For most firms, they are:

1) Real estate/leases
2) Talent
3) Technology, and
4) MBDCS (For example, consider whether formalizing remote work options for more employees could save on number 1 above.)

Another way to save costs is to use and apply the "Re-s" to save costs and expenses. What are the Re-s? Review, re-budget, renegotiate, retool, reuse, refine, refocus, repurpose, recycle, resell, rewrite, etc. The idea is to leverage and make more out of what already are sunk costs and what already exists.

There are many other ways to optimize and save costs and expenses, several of which are described in this book, and there are many other resources available on this subject. Detailed cost-control measures are not a focus of this book.

Instead, below are tried-and-true ways for firms and practitioners to strategically assess their current reality and situation in a methodical manner in order to make the best possible strategic decisions—beyond simply saving expenses—during the full course of an economic downturn.

Why formally assess the competitive position of your firm or practice?

The purpose of conducting a formal assessment of your firm and practice is to drive profitable growth by determining:

1. Who you are now (from both your internal perspective and your clients' perspective).
2. Who you want to and realistically can become based on who you are now.
3. Exactly how—over time—you expect to accomplish the changes or transformation.

Any meaningful assessment uses data and metrics, which provide needed focus and discipline of action and are extremely useful in measuring progress and performance. If there is an aversion to metrics within your firm, it must be overcome by educating owners about what metrics mean and do not mean. Of course, all data has flaws, but it must be gathered, normalized, used and analyzed in order to conduct a meaningful assessment.

Also, the current competitive position of any professional services firm and any individual practitioner can only be validly assessed by considering and evaluating **both** the firm's perspective/position and the client's perspective/position. Do not make the mistake of conducting only an internal assessment, during and after a pandemic, because the client's perspective, situation, and needs are everything. We know the most valuable asset to your firm and practice is PEOPLE–both internally with the firm and externally—so be sure to assess both.

How to conduct a formal, strategic competitive assessment

First, set aside dedicated time to formally assess your current competitive position. Avoid conducting the assessment alone. Create a team, committee, or working group not only to quickly gather the needed information, but so there are various and diverse perspectives involved. If your firm has a chief value officer or another executive whose job largely consists of communicating with and interviewing clients, be sure to include them.

Work individually, assign a dedicated team, and/or retain an experienced expert(s) to gather, assemble (into spreadsheets or otherwise), and then analyze the critical information below.

Gather key information & data: As fast as possible, gather the information below and then calculate and tally it by firm, practice area/groups/department, and if offices are formal profit centers, by office, too.

The most important thing to assess and stay on top of during and after a pandemic is your clients. As discussed earlier, without them, there is no work to do and survival is not an option.

Firm information and data to gather:

- ✓ List and calculate how many and which clients make up 25%, 50%, and 80% of total revenues for the last year and three years cumulative.
- ✓ Calculate what percentage of your total revenue comes from your largest 25 to 50 clients.
- ✓ Identify the best, nonactive, past clients who may hire you again in the future.
- ✓ Inventory and identify top referral sources who could refer more or other types of work to you or your firm.
- ✓ Create a spreadsheet and define each client (or the clients who make up 50% of your revenue) by:
  - Title, role, position and/or decision-making authority
  - Main location/headquarters and other key demographics
  - Industry
  - Type and amount of firm practice types used
  - Level of sophistication of each type of work (e.g., commodity, experience, bet the company/crucial to the organization, etc.)
  - Length of relationship with you or your firm

- Strength of relationship (e.g. sole source, strong, average, can use improvement, etc.)
- Other firms work for client by type and volume.
- Your billing rates versus competitors' rates (local, regional, and global as relevant).
- Average total fees you charge by type of engagement, case, problem, matter, or sector as relevant.

✓ Assess the type of client and stage each client is in:
- As a result of the pandemic (i.e., booming, struggling, flatlining).
- Clients lifecycle (e.g., launch, growth, diversification, mature, decline, exit).
- Type of buyer (e.g., all work is outsourced, specific areas, volume, one-off, etc.).
- Level of maturity of your relationship with each client is by duration, intensity, quality, lifetime value, etc.

✓ Mark those that represent the opportunity to:
- Enhance the relationship
- Do more of the same work you have done for them to date
- Have other types of work you could do for them
- Can refer more of other types of work to you/your firm

Firm or Practice Revenue Trends:

✓ Select an appropriate time interval (e.g., the last three to five years).

✓ Define all revenues in 20% tranches by client name; practice area, type or group used; by office; and, if relevant, by leader relationship partner.
- Number of clients with annual revenues in relevant size intervals.
- Percentage of total firm and practice group revenues coming from top 20% of clients.

- Total revenue based on internal referrals between practice groups, and other related data.
- Total revenue from responses to requests for proposal/information/qualifications (RFP?Q/I).
- Total revenue received based on discounts, fixed/flat fees or other alternative fee arrangements (AFAs).

✓ Define your market(s) and specialization(s). (Refer back to Chapter 7 and Appendix 1 for more information).

✓ List the depth of practice/practice group experience in size, geographic reach, and scale.

Analyze all operating costs and expenses as described above and, where possible, benchmark them against competitors.

The above internal information and data will allow you to methodically determine your current competitive position and determine where the best opportunities are. For example:

- What work that you do is most in demand and from which clients and markets? You may need to retool, reshuffle, or redirect some fee-earners to do the work most in demand, and in areas where demand will develop (i.e., workouts and bankruptcy).
- Is there enough diversification and balance in your client/work portfolio between cyclical and counter-cyclical services and practices to fill needs in both growing and contracting economies?
- If over 70% of your revenue comes from a single client, the best strategic choice will be to do all you can to maintain and secure that relationship, while also working to build and enhance it. At the same time, consider the best strategic ways to increase and diversify your client base.
- If your firm has many separate physical offices and you do not know or measure profitability by office, now is the time to do so. Why? Because post-pandemic, reducing real estate and lease

expenses by moving relevant employees to remote operations is a viable new option.

From the client's perspective, gather and identify the sources of competitive advantage(s) and disadvantage(s) for the firm and practice types/groups.

At all costs, avoid presuming or assuming you already know your clients' situations, what they think, how and why they buy, their situation, and their perspective. Without gathering and assessing consistent information from your clients, referral sources, and other key stakeholders, a competitive assessment is not bona fide, meaningful, or useful to help you survive and thrive.

Audrey Rubin, JD, who recently served as Vice President and C.O.O. of Aon Corporation's Global Law and Compliance Department, where she was responsible for all technology, budget, diversity, strategic planning, and process improvement, says, "Clients are continually becoming more sophisticated and selective when hiring outside professional services firms. Firms need to start obtaining valid client input before making strategic decisions because the clients' perspective is critical. Yet, most law firms tend to make strategic decisions without consulting their clients at all, or by just informally asking a few clients what they think. As a result, firms are missing details and nuances that could enhance or improve their strategic investments and decisions." More ways to gather client feedback are described in the next chapter.

Gathering critical external information and data

When is the last time you or your firm conducted an organized, statistically valid Client Survey, then tallied, analyzed, and utilized the results? If you have never conducted such a survey, now is the time. But, be sure to plan the survey to be as brief and least intrusive to clients as possible during challenging times.

Consider mimicking a best practice used by an AmLaw 100 firm, whose managing partner works with the firm's other leaders and business development and client service team to create a list of three to five questions to ask all key clients. Firm staff inserts the questions into a spreadsheet, then the managing partner sends it (along with a cover memo describing why, what, and how to) to all practice group heads, asking them to have all key partners in their practice groups call each of their top-five clients personally and fill in the spreadsheet with their responses. Once completed, all responses are sent to a point person within the firm, who tallies and reports the results to firm management. This is an efficient procedure in a large firm that allows firm leaders to have relevant information about their clients' perspectives in a valid and useable manner.

Individual professional services providers can do the same thing, i.e., come up with three to five key questions to ask each of their best clients and referral sources, make the calls, tally and track all responses, and then analyze and use the information to assess their competitive position.

Some key issues to consider asking clients and referral sources about include:

- From the client's perspective, ask them what they think are your competitive advantage(s) and disadvantage(s) for you, the firm, and/or practice types/groups.
- Ask about you or your firm's reputation. Ask them to assign you a rating as compared to other professionals they use in your space/practice type.
- Ask what they think of when they hear your firm or your name. Ask them about brand associations/attributes, i.e., when you think of me/my firm, how would you describe it? What comes to mind?

Other possible issues to ask or post to clients about appear in the chart below.

Client Experience & Satisfaction Criteria	Rating (Scale 1-10, with 10 highest)
Clearly communicates options, expectations, fees and costs before starting work	
Initiates and provides regular updates throughout representation/engagement	
Quickly responds to questions and requests	
Provides enough information to make you feel knowledgeable and prepared	
Schedules calls and meetings when convenient for you	
Responds quickly to my/our communications and requests	
All professionals and staff you worked with were professional, courteous and friendly	
Initiates periodic, unpromoted, proactive communications	
Provides value for the amount charged for the results and service delivered	
Easy to do business with	
Makes you feel your business is valued	

Once gathered in a measurable manner, you can analyze the above information to determine strategic and tactical choices that will best help you or your firm survive and thrive.

For example, use the information and data above to ask yourself:

- Which clients have not been particularly hard hit in this economy? Come up with and offer a short-term or permanent billing, fee or costs alternative(s). Doing so will go a long way in providing services in alignment with what the market will bear and will also help build goodwill and your reputation.

- What service(s) do I provide routinely and repetitively where clients may prefer to pay a fixed fee or an alternative to the billable hour? Some elements of most cases, engagements and transactions can be replicated, serviced, and delivered at a lower total fee than the traditional billable hour model.

- What do most of my clients value highest? What do they need and want but is still not being delivered?

The results from client surveys can also help you precisely define and communicate your unique competitive position, also known as a value proposition. For most professional services providers, their unique value proposition is a combination of who they serve; what problems they solve/solutions they provide; what is truly unique about them as a professional; how solutions/services are delivered; how they communicate and charge for services rendered.

The value proposition for each firm and practitioner varies depending on many factors and should be defined as specifically as possible. For example, "providing quality, cost-effective services" is not a specific or unique value proposition, because every firm and practitioner stake this same claim.

Create and implement a process to review your competitive position and prioritize

Once a formal competitive assessment is completed, it's important to review, discuss, consider, and decide upon which strategic choices will be best for your firm or practices, and then prioritize them.

Below is a process and procedure used by several leading firms to prioritize and make strategic decisions.

- Assemble a team of key stakeholders (and possibly a trusted, objective, and diverse outside advisor with no ties to the outcome(s)) to reflect, consider, and brainstorm all current projects and work. Appoint a scribe to list and inventory everything that could, should, or needs to be done by project name and main person responsible. Make sure to create a list in writing or better yet compile into a spreadsheet.

- Mark each project by:
  - Level of importance/potential value/ROI to firm or clients
  - Level of urgency

- Using a scale from 1-10, with 10 being the highest, assign a rank to each project by the total amount of estimated work and effort each will take.

- Consider and mark which projects to eliminate, cut, refine, re-scope or re-consider. If more work needs to be done to re-scope the project, assign one professional to do so.

- Conduct any additional analysis or review, then collate all top-priority projects and work.

- Formally assign one key professional to own, oversee, manage, and implement each priority project or work stream.

- Create metric and data-drive reporting and communications procedures and processes. The results and strategic initiatives decided upon as part of the assessment process must be regularly reported upon and communicated or will quickly fail.

- Schedule regular reviews and a check-in process because uncertainty and change are given. Know that priorities will change, often when you least expect them to.

- Be prepared and ready to re-evaluate priorities. Continual change is a reality, so the need to be flexible and adaptable and to do so quickly is very important.

Formal assessments—whether conducted periodically (every two to three years) or annually—is a business discipline all professional services firms and practitioners need to adopt. Do not just conduct a formal assessment once, at a single point in time. Instead, institutionalize the assessment process (on an annual or every two to three years' basis) as a continual, on-going necessity needed to survive and thrive. Formal assessments are needed to optimize operations, performance, and profitability, and to remain profitable.

The key to long-term success and profitability is to regularly review and assess the competitive position of your firm, department, or practice in a meaningful manner. Then invest time, effort, and money routinely and strategically in both good and bad economies to keep up with and/or surpass competition in key markets and/or client segments.

To continue profitable growth and to develop your primary assets (which are *you*, your clients, referral sources, partners, and staff), every professional must make strategic investments in key areas. Identify which strategic investments will yield the best return on investment, then make the time to implement and follow-up upon them.

Once a thorough competitive assessment has been completed, it is time to review, analyze, and brainstorm the results with a diverse team of stakeholders, executives, and one or more experienced, outside, and independent experts.

Key Takeaways

- ➤ Embrace, institutionalize and schedule a formal strategic assessment of your practice, group, department or firm, ideally once a year.
- ➤ Create a defined assessment process, including roles, responsibilities, due dates, reporting, reviews, and communications.
- ➤ Identify and gather all needed and desired information and data from both internal and external sources.
- ➤ Involve a variety of perspectives in the analysis and discussion of the resulting information and your strategic options (which are described in the next chapter).

10

CONSIDER & MAKE STRATEGIC CHOICES & DECISIONS

> The firms and practitioners who continuously and strategically adapt to evolving realities will own the future.
>
> – Gerry Riskin

In a post-pandemic world, strategic decisions and choices must be made quickly to optimally allocate and deploy your resources. Time is of the essence.

In order to survive, grow, and thrive, all firms and practitioners must continue to invest time, money, and effort into their practice. The key is to do so strategically. Prior studies from previous recessions show professional services firms that continued to invest during the economic downturns experienced the greatest growth in profits during the recovery.

Due to the speed at which information now travels and the pace at which change occurs, in order to survive and thrive, strategic assessment and choices need to be made much faster, more efficiently, and more effectively than in the past.

Every firm leader and practitioner must balance their attention between reacting to the immediate needs, problems, developments, and issues while being sure to allocate time to carefully plan ahead to ensure business continuity. The need to accelerate strategic actions can be a matter of survival.

The best strategic choices focus on and maximize your strengths, while also focusing on the best opportunities (ideally identified using a formal assessment as described in Chapter 9).

Think (again) about what you most want to be known and remembered for. Consider social and corporate responsibility, profitability with purpose, radical or just average generosity, and, most importantly, the new relationship reality.

As emphasized throughout this book, all professional services revolve around people, so firms and practitioners need to continue to strategically communicate with all stakeholders and target markets. As mentioned, don't make the mistake of cutting costs to the bone and stopping all MBDCS investments. Ralph Baxter says, "Now is the time to focus on how you and your firm can do what you do *better*."[45]

Overall, clients remain less than fully satisfied with outside professional services providers and firms. Clients perceive inconsistencies, redundancies, inefficiencies and wasted efforts, too much reaction, not enough unpromoted, provider-initiated communications, and too much cost and expense. So, there is significant room for improvement, which requires strategy, tactics, implementation and follow-up.

To be effective, *any* strategy or tactic designed to grow a firm, group, or individual practice must involve the right mix of:

* **People** (both fee-earners and other business and professional staff)
* **Processes/procedures** (who will do what, when, and related metrics)
* **Technology** (efficiently access, track, and report data and information)

Be prepared to pivot and retool *fast*

When the economy comes to a standstill, as it did during the 2020 crisis, uncertainty abounds. That puts a premium on flexibility for firms and professional services providers to react quickly to economic, market, client-related and business changes.

Being forced to create fully operational, remote workplaces was a sea change for many professional services firms and providers who were used to going into their (often fancy) offices to work each day. The question post-2020 pandemic is whether remote work will become more the norm once the crisis passes. It is important that all firms and practitioners be fully ready and able to work remotely at any time in the future. "When social distancing guidelines and shelter-in-place directives are widespread, all organizations must adapt by adopting fully-functional, virtual workspaces to replace on-site meetings and reviews," says John Reikes, Vice President, Disputes and Investigations at Elevate Services (https://elevateservices.com/).

As compared to the largest companies in the world and the world's largest professional services firms, most other professional services firms have extremely limited available budgets and time. So, in economic downturns, launching a bold initiative such as entering a new market, opening a new office, or acquiring laterals can impact strategic maneuverability and sap resources and reserves. It's important to make strategic decisions and choices carefully.

Now and throughout history, disease, epidemics, and pandemics have been and still are a part of life.[46]

Graphic as of May 1, 2020

As a result, we all need to expect they will occur again and be prepared and ready, both personally and professionally. For those accustomed to going into a physical office space every day, the transition to remote work was not easy. Here is a real-life example of a professional services provider who was prepared and acted quickly to respond to the 2020 crisis:

Like many of us, as the 2020 crisis was developing, Jeff Morris, LL.B., a Toronto-based mediator of business, commercial, and insurance disputes, who has practiced law for over thirty-eight years, was closely watching and thinking about the impact the crisis would have on his mediation practice.

Prior to March 2020, Jeff had not used any online or virtual tools to conduct mediations or do any work at all. As is the case for most lawyers, much of his work was conducted at various office locations, with all parties meeting physically in person. But, by late February 2020, Jeff realized he needed a contingency plan to be able to continue providing his mediation services without using the normal method of meeting physically in person with the parties.

By early March 2020, Jeff went into overdrive, crafting his contingency plan and then beginning to build and develop it. His plan included:

- ✓ Finding a user-friendly, secure, online platform that would allow many parties to meet virtually in one space. Depending on security and encryption levels required, Jeff now uses either Zoom, WebEx, or Microsoft Teams for his mediations.

- ✓ Setting up and securing each platform for his practice.

- ✓ Drafting a comprehensive mediation protocol and process map plus user guides for his clients and parties.

- ✓ Creating a YouTube video explaining how to mediate online.

- ✓ Sending the above information to his current clients, past clients, and referral sources.

The result? In less than two weeks after completing and launching his contingency plan, Jeff had scheduled and conducted eight online mediations using his new delivery method. But Jeff also continues to innovate and adapt to the new normal. He recently registered a new domain name, zoommediations.com, and created a plan to expand his meditation practice to resolve international disputes between U.S.- and U.K.-based companies, by serving as a neutral, Canadian-based licensed mediator.

Making any strategic choice requires taking some level of risk

If we have learned anything over the course of the 2020 pandemic, it's that 100% control is an illusion. None of us have any control over many things. But a basic human need is to create a sense of control in the way we chose to spend our time, our habits, and choices, etc. It's important to remember (at least in the back of your mind) that true control over everything in your life, practice, and world is a mirage. As a result, we each need to decide what strategic and measured risks to take to maintain and develop our professional services firm, profession, and/or career.

To one degree or another, risk exists in every aspect of life. Business risks are real and especially significant in the current economic environment. Many licensed professionals, including lawyers, accountants, actuaries, and many others, are often hired and paid to eliminate, reduce, and/or mitigate risks.

All bona fide strategies require a choice, i.e., choosing one thing over another. By definition, that means ignoring or missing something else (which also comes with an opportunity cost). So, strategic direction is, in essence, the half of the glass that is full; that half you or your firm have chosen to invest time and resources into.

Upgrading the way you assess, analyze, and evaluate risks can benefit your firm and practice. Consider getting different perspectives before making strategic choices, especially from your most valuable existing clients and referral sources, but also from others who are independent or do not have a stake in the decision or who have different experiences or backgrounds. New perspectives usually provide insights and value.

Below is a chart to use to enhance the evaluation of the inevitable risks involved with any strategic decision. Remember also to carefully consider the risks and potential short-, medium-, and long-term cost(s) of doing nothing and maintaining the status quo.

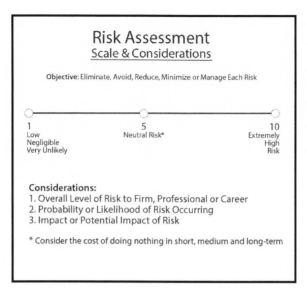

It's also important to create and use an objective method to determine the impact of strategic choices and to prioritize them. The two following charts may help.

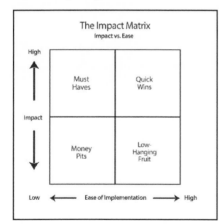

Once you start to meaningfully reflect on your current situation and strategic choices, remember: the importance of *people* to the survival and growth or any professional services firm or practice cannot be over-estimated.

The trick is to assess and make strategic choices around the two main sets of people most important to your practice:

1. **Internal stakeholders.** Including fee-earners and all professional and business support staff, down to the janitor and receptionist(s). Every single person who works for and with your firm plays a role in serving both internal and external stakeholders to maintain and grow the firm and practice. A common mistake made by many highly educated professional services leaders and providers is they *assume* or *presume* they already know everything there is to know about both crucial groups of people: internal and external stakeholders. Yet, it is proven that gathering informal and formal input from both groups helps a firm survive and thrive over time.

2. **External stakeholders.** Consider the entire ecosystem of those people who do not work directly in your firm—not just clients, but referral sources, vendors, experts, etc. Work to avoid assuming or presuming you already know everything there is to know about them.

Great questions to ask yourself: "Where is my firm/practice most vulnerable?" and "What is the 'glue' that hold us together as a firm?"

Direct strategic choices there.

The #1 goal and objective should be to enhance your relationships with key people and stakeholders

If PEOPLE are the most valuable asset, it stands to reason that doing everything strategically viable to secure, maintain, enhance, improve, and develop your relationships with key stakeholders involved in your firm and practice is the best investment of time, money, and effort. Now is the time to invest in getting much closer to your clients, referral sources, staff, colleagues, and other firm, professional, and practice-related stakeholders.

The value and use of client/stakeholder feedback and strategic options

Using the client's perspective when making strategic decisions is crucial for many reasons already described in this book. But what are some of the other benefits of regularly gathering and using meaningful client feedback to run a firm or practice?

Investing in client feedback can improve your understanding and knowledge about your clients to improve service, client satisfaction, and experience with you and your firm; strengthen your relationships; increase referrals; provide competitive advantage by knowing what's around the corner to proactively anticipate their needs; enhance the client's perception of value they receive from you and your firm; increase your Net Promoter Score; and numerous studies have proven it can boost the bottom line.

Unfortunately, most law firms and other professional services firms and individual professional services providers still rely only and mainly on informal, anecdotal client feedback not supported by data. An example of informal and anecdotal feedback is when, for example, a client or referral source says or emails a lawyer or fee-earner something complimentary about the results or service the lawyer/firm provided or about the level of responsiveness of the firm's associates, colleagues, or staff, and then that lawyer or fee-earner relays that feedback to their partners or leaders, usually verbally. The problem is, once the feedback is received and/or relayed, it is not usually acted upon in any other way. It's usually quickly forgotten. This is not to suggest such informal, anecdotal feedback is not important. It is *very* important. But, know that the law firms that attain "Client Service A-Team" rankings and status in BTI Consulting's annual report rely on much more than informal, anecdotal client feedback.

So, the problems associated with relying only on informal client feedback is that it does not necessarily 1) include what all or most clients think and experience, or 2) capture client feedback in a consistent, representative, statistically valid, or useful manner. As a result, relying on informal client feedback is not complete or thorough information on which to rely when assessing your competitive position and making the best strategic choices in the future.

Some professional services firms and individual providers have already proactively institutionalized a routine client feedback procedure and process designed to assess and measure the law firm's or practitioner's performance. Examples include:

❖ **"After Action Review" (AAR)**[47]. Some (but few) firms and practitioners regularly conduct an AAR upon or shortly after the conclusion of every or most engagements, matters or cases. AARs are most often conducted verbally by phone or in-person. They are sometimes conducted using a brief email or survey like the below:

Client Experience & Satisfaction Criteria	Rating (Scale 1-10, with 10 highest)
Clearly communicates options, expectations, fees and costs before starting work	
Initiates and provides regular updates throughout representation/engagement	
Quickly responds to questions and requests	
Provides enough information to make you feel knowledgeable and prepared	
Schedules calls and meetings when convenient for you	
Responds quickly to my/our communications and requests	
All professionals and staff you worked with were professional, courteous and friendly	
Initiates periodic, unpromoted, proactive communications	
Provides value for the amount charged for the results and service delivered	
Easy to do business with	
Makes you feel your business is valued	

❖ **Client Interviews/Client Reviews. Even before 2020,** more professional services firms and individual professional services providers began regularly conducting client interviews and client reviews, either annually or periodically. These formal client reviews are usually planned, conducted and followed up upon by a mix of professionals such as the firm's CEO or managing partner, the firm's chief value or service officer, the firm's lead relationship partner for each client, and/or a qualified outside vendor. Some firms and practitioners conduct them mainly or only with their top, key, or most important clients, while others regularly interview a representative sample of clients by type, practice area, revenue tranche, or other criteria. A few firms maintain automated, internal client scoreboards that report all client feedback from the various feedback tools used by the firm and consider these scores as part of the compensation process.

While having a formal client interview or review program is commendable and helpful, an outstanding issue for many firms and practitioners that do currently use them is that not all firms have a formal process in place to:

1) Ask the same/similar questions

2) Tally and track all responses in an organized system or

3) Measure and evaluate all responses in an organized, consistent, or meaningful manner.

In addition, many firms do not:

1) Act upon the client feedback or

2) Follow-up with clients to inform them of any adjustments or changes made because of their feedback.

If this is the case for your firm or practice, now is the time to consider making upgrades and enhancements to your existing client review process, so you can gather and use the information gained most productively in your efforts to survive and thrive in the future.

Key Client Programs

In the ten years leading up to the 2020 crisis, many major firms formalized, instituted, and consistently funded strategic Key Client Programs and the results are impressive. A few firms have seen their "client share" (i.e., the percentage of the client's total outside spend on services that goes to that firm) grow as much as ten to thirty percent. Since it costs approximately half as much to develop business from existing clients than from new ones and these dollars translate to the bottom line more efficiently, this is a solid, proven growth strategy.

Not all firms are seeing these kinds of measurable results from their Key Client Program, mainly because they make only a small or point-in-time investment (i.e., are not making continual efforts and investments). Other firms make an investment in a Key Client Program but do so "on the cheap," which means their people, existing processes, and systems cannot support sustainable efforts and therefore produce little or mediocre results from the firm's investment. Key Client Programs are only successful in law firms where they are supported by culture, leadership, compensation systems, personnel, and other factors.

Client Mapping is a diagnostic tool focused not on the firm's or practitioner's performance but rather on the client's perceptions and experience with the firm, practitioners, facilities, technologies, and staff. Client mapping consists of formally defining or listing your client's journey, touchpoints, experience, and value chain in a step-by-step format, using a process orientation.

As a result of the 2020 crisis, client, customer, employee, and other stakeholder *touch points* have dramatically changed. Now is the time to assess, map, and upgrade them. Doing so may require mapping them, getting up to speed, training, and/or personalized coaching.

What's OUT (as of May 2020):
1. Handshakes and hugs.
2. Meetings held physically in-person (PIP).
3. Large scale PIP events, conferences, seminars

What's IN:
1. Staying six to fifteen feet away from other people when out in public or at work
2. Online, virtual communications of all types, especially:
   - Emails
   - Telephone calls
   - Messaging apps

- Video calls, conferences, and meetings
- Virtual webinars, seminars, conferences, and events

Pre-pandemic, very few professional services firms or practitioners had taken the time to define a client touchpoint map for their firm or practice.

Remember: all clients' journeys start well before there is an initial contact, so Internet presence, SEO rankings, keywords, and the appearance, ease-of-use, and utility of the firm's website are critical. But, once a contact has been made, what are the most common touchpoints during a client's journey?

Examples of common touchpoints that all clients or referral sources looking to use and hire outside professional services include (but are not limited to) the quality of:

- The initial contact (whether by phone, in person, electronic communication or walk-in)

- The initial prospective client meeting, setting expectations and associated follow up

- Conflicts review and clearing process

- Engagement/case/matter assessment and scoping

- Pricing, billing and invoicing options and formats

- Retainer/engagement/welcome letter and process

- Turn-away communications and letter

- Office visits, including directions, parking, facilities

- Remote communications options, access, how tos, etc.

- Other important touchpoints that occur over the duration of any engagement, matter, or case.

An example of how touchpoints has changed due to the 2020 crisis, almost all professional services firms with physical offices had to design a re-opening plan and re-entry strategy for employees, clients, and all other visitors. This necessity illustrates, for one thing, how it would be highly beneficial (maybe essential) to use a formal process mapping approach that involves your diverse set of key stakeholders and other thinkers, in order to consider and brainstorm re-entry from all the essential "people" perspectives: the employee, the client, the visitor, and maybe service providers for the firms, as well.

Doing so creates a more consistent re-entry experience and journey, which contains many touchpoints (at a safe social distance) all designed around making people feel that entering and spending time at the firm's office is safe and sanitary.

Another common touchpoint all clients experience is the intake process with the provider and firm, which consists of many communications over an interval of time.

For example, every client received an engagement/retainer letter from the firm to review and sign before work can commence. It annoys many clients when a firm sends engagement/retainer letters that include a standard clause defining an automatic, advance waiver of any future conflicts once the letter is signed.

Jeff Carr says, "I suggest all firms review and edit their engagement and retainer letters to eliminate all text that refers to an automatic, in-advance waiver of conflicts. All conflicts must be considered and evaluated individually, so you need to call your client to discuss them on a case-by-case basis."

Jeff also suggests, "Create budgets for all your work—every engagement, case, or matter—even if budgets are not required or asked for by the client. Review the budget with the client, which will allow you to get even greater clarity into the client's expectations and objectives. Due to the intense competition among outside service providers, those who do not make and adhere to budgets and SOPs (standard operating procedures) will become increasingly less busy."

If you are thinking that formally mapping your client's experience or journey would deliver additional competitive benefits for your practice, keep in mind that process improvement and project management are two different yet related business disciplines.

Process improvement helps determine the best way to carry out a type or certain kind of work or task to achieve efficiencies, consistencies, excellence in the quality of work and service, increases in the probability of a successful outcome(s), and predictability.

Project management is a role and set of skills that ensures the "best process" is defined and used appropriately, and there is active management of schedules, staff, and deliverables throughout a project, engagement, or matter.[48]

Some of the steps required in the process to map the client's journey effectively are:

- Assemble a diverse team, and appoint a lead facilitator, note-taker, and owner of this mapping project (often, involving an experienced, outside facilitator, client service expert, and process mapper can add value).

- Define the issue, why it needs to be mapped, and the benefits of doing so.

- Measure or assess the current performance of the process (which is hard to do in any measurable manner without first obtaining consistent and meaningful client feedback).

- List the primary, most important, main, or all touchpoints or steps in the process.

- Include decision and review points, along with relevant data on costs, timing, average turnaround, and other key metrics for each step.

- Identify and list the best possible ways to measure results or improvements of each step (as is possible).

- Review the map from several perspectives to ensure it is approximately 80% complete.

- Analyze the opportunities to reduce waste, redundancies, and/or variations.

- Improve the process by identifying, implementing, and validating changes.

- Control the process by implementing methods to ensure improvements will be sustainable.

For more ways firms and individual practitioners can expand key client and referral source relationships, see these recent articles I wrote:

- ❖ www.law.com/2019/04/08/best-ways-to-expand-key-client-relationships-from-the-lawyers-and-firms-perspectives/

- ❖ www.lawjournalnewsletters.com/2019/05/01/best-ways-to-expand-key-client-relationships/.

Precisely define your target markets

If you do not have all your target markets formally defined in writing, now is the time to do so. Why? Because without formal market definition, many MBDCS efforts do not attain any results and are not necessarily optimized. Specific market-defining criteria can be found in Chapter 7 and in Appendix 1.

If your firm or practice is not yet internally organized and operating under an industry or niche (as defined by the client's perspective) structure or matrix, now is the time to reorganize the firm, its practice groups, or departments using a matrix structure, as appropriate.[49]

It is not enough to simply have industries, specialty areas, or niches listed on your firm's website or biographical sketch. There must be internal coordination and collaboration to support and drive the groups and, most importantly, a go-to-market strategic plan for each, including the most appropriate and effective MBDCS tools to deploy (see the list in Chapter 7).

Increase your commitment to and investments in technology, innovation, research, and development

Now is the time for all firms and practitioners to get more serious about technology, innovation, and R&D in an organized, strategic, productive, and most potentially profitable manner.

Ask yourself:

> ➤ "What strategic choices or changes would make the most positive impact on my practice?"

> ➤ "What do I have, what do I offer, what else is needed in my area of practice?"

> ➤ "What else can I sell that is needed, adds value, and is affordable (or not)?"

> Effectively adopting proven, new technologies ahead of or in pace with competitors will be critical to future success.
>
> – Gerry Riskin

Assess your current technology(ies), related skills, how it impacts and is used by key stakeholders, and identify gaps

By necessity, the 2020 crisis led the digital transformation of many professional services firms, practices, and other businesses. Consider how many professionals rarely used video-conferencing and remote or telework who were forced to do so because of the pandemic. The only question is whether these changes, adaptations, and improvements, brought about so suddenly by the crisis, will stick, become permanent, and/or be expanded upon, or whether firms and practitioners will fight to revert back to what was "business as usual" or considered "normal" (as they defined "business as usual" or "normal" before the crisis hit). Continually assessing use of modern and proven technologies for all types of professions and firms is a must in order to thrive in the future.

This Twitter posts sums up the technological changes thrust upon the practice of law from the 2020 crisis:

In a related and trending post on LinkedIn, Olga Mack, CEO of Parley Pro, posted a video that summarizes the impacts of the 2020 crisis to date.[50] It provides answers to these questions: "1) Who is responsible for your firm/organization's accelerated flexible working arrangements? 2) Advanced digital evolution? 3} Who championed collaboration? 4) Who pioneered adoption of modern enterprise tools? And 5) Who impacted your organization the most?" The answer to each of these questions in the video is the global pandemic (not the organization's CEO, COO, Board, or any other executive).

Even before the 2020 crisis forced remote work on a scale and scope never known, many traditionally run law firms and other professional services firms and individual practices were and still are in dire need of technology update(s).

The need to stay current with the use of relevant, time saving, and productivity-boosting technology to support your practice has never been greater. No firm or provider wants to be out-paced and out-priced by competitors. Many modern technologies now provide firms and practitioners with outcome-driven solutions that make workflows more time- and cost-efficient. Some firms and professionals have already been procuring and adopting new, more modern technologies, but not enough.

Ron Friedmann, a leading observer, and commentator on the legal and professional services sectors, made some predictions in a recent blog post. In the post, Ron projects what things there will be MORE of because of the crisis. He suggests there will be MORE: remote work from home; use of secure clouds; remote document review; use of deal management platforms; use of chatbots for concierge firm and client service; and defined workflows and processes.[51]

Howard "Bud" Phillips, Chief Information Officer, Elevate Services (https://elevateservices.com), says, "Deploying the right technology and services that markedly boost how fast and efficiently firms respond will pay dividends long into the future. Look to institute flexible solutions that allow adjustments as conditions evolve."

Gabriel Teninbaum has these suggestions for every professional services firm and provider:

1. **Learn.** The first step in identifying ways to be more efficient, effective, and/or innovative is having a roadmap for doing so. Every organization should appoint a trusted team member (a partner, a manager, or another executive) to learn about the tools and techniques that are changing legal work. This can be accomplished through a formal course of study (like the legaltechcertificate.com program that I oversee at Suffolk Law), tech CLEs, or regularly reading blogs and newsletters that cover legal tech developments.

2. **Build something**. Remember that book, *Shop Class as Soulcraft*? Its premise is that building things is a meaningful and motivating experience. It almost doesn't matter what you build (but starting points like making a simple expert system, a calculator on Excel, or even a checklist of procedures to pass along to staff is a good starting place), so long as it's useful and you work through the process.[52]

One example of where modern technology creates efficiencies and minimizes risk for firms is in the area of new client intake. Many firms still clear conflicts by sending mass emails around to all fee-earners in the firm. This approach is risky because it is not necessarily complete or thorough. Firms that have not yet formalized their internal client selection criteria and conflict review programs may be lagging competitors.

It is imperative to have a careful, internal review prior to intake of new clients because traditional legal conflicts are no longer simple and straightforward. Most clients of professional services firms now generate myriad business conflicts that need to be carefully studied and sorted out before intake. Most major professional services firms now have an internal general counsel (GC) or committee, whose task is to make a careful review of all potential new clients before intake. Unfortunately, too many firms have the GC appointed without appropriate internal coordination procedures, processes, systems, criteria, and/or technology to support effective intake analysis (a problem that also impacts the firm's MBDCS efforts and department).

John Sharkey, who serves as Vice President, Risk Practice Group at Intapp (www.intapp.com), said, "Research has shown that professional services firms experience a significant business challenge within the risk and compliance process of client onboarding, resulting in revenue and opportunity losses. Modern firms now have a centralized clearance function supported by sophisticated technology to help accelerate and streamline the intake processes, saving time and improving the efficiency of how conflicts are handled."

For firms or individual practitioners who lag behind the modern technology adoption curve, consider this advice from Colin Levy, Corporate Counsel at Salary.com, a leading voice on legal technology and innovation. On LinkedIn, he posted:

1. Deploying technology will not do you much good unless you have a) a clear idea of your users' adaptability and openness to using tech, b) know the specific problem you are trying to solve, and c) know the processes you currently use and who is involved in those processes.

2. Technology and innovation are not the same thing. In some ways, they are connected, but they are not mutually dependent on one another.

3. In legal, there is a clear communication gap between law firms/law departments and clients as well as legal tech vendors. There is a need for folks who can help bridge this gap. Count me as one of those individuals.[53]

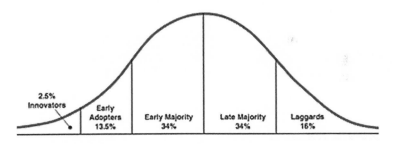

One example of large-scale technology solutions for professional services firms comes from Intapp (www.intapp.com/intapp-oneplace), which offers a suite of technology solutions designed specifically for the needs of professional services firms such as law, accounting, consulting, and financial services firms. A large percentage of the world's largest law firms and other leading professional services firms have turned to Intapp's solutions, which connect disparate systems containing siloed data into one cohesive platform, thus saving time, and creating many other efficiencies.

The non-profit group Corporate Legal Operations Consortium (CLOC; https://cloc.org) is a relatively new and rapidly growing group of legal operations professionals, many of whom work in corporate/organization legal departments, but many law firms are also CLOC members. CLOC supports their members in their use of the plethora of proven technologies available to support the practice of law and legal operations.

CLOC has experienced exponential growth in recent years because of the dramatic increase in the types and numbers of new technologies and their adoption, which has created the need to hire staff to vet, enable, implement, and manage them for a firm or legal department. The entire legal operations market and ecosystem is growing so rapidly that CLOC recently launched a Legal Ops Directory (https://directory.cloc.org) of vendors for law firms, legal departments, and lawyers to identify possible technologies to consider. If your firm is considering evaluating and procuring new, more modern technology(ies), the CLOC directory is a great resource.

Connie Brenton, who serves as Chief of Staff and Senior Director of Legal Operations at NetApp (www.netapp.com), says, "A major objective for many legal departments is to use the right legal resource—the right provider at the right price with the right level of quality. There is tremendous opportunity for outside lawyers and firms to proactively suggest innovative approaches to achieve this objective. A few areas deserving attention and strategic and operational input from law firms and alternative legal service providers include artificial intelligence (AI), pre-litigation and e-discovery processes, streamlining data privacy compliance, and leveraging technology to automate legal activities and tasks."

During both good times and bad, assessing and making upgrades and changes to your use of modern, up-to-date technologies is critical to staying competitive and relevant.

Innovation—upgrade your focus and pace

Innovating does not have to be complex. Instead, think about simple things that can be done to maximize your productivity, service quality and delivery, and MBDCS.

A simple innovation any practitioner or firm can make is to start to formally capture and track any client complaints, issues, or bottlenecks, but few do so. Instead, within most firms, complaints are either not really heard or are minimized or ignored. Without tracking them, there is no way to escalate or manage a continual improvement process in your firm and practice.

For example, many clients would like and prefer customized formatting changes to the firm's standard invoice template. A common client complaint is that there is no "cumulative fees to date" for ongoing matters, engagements, or cases on invoices. The standard format of most firms' invoices does not include such a line item. This causes clients to have to take time to manually calculate fees-to-date, which wastes their valuable time. Making that simple change to all invoices would be a small but welcome innovation from the clients' perspective.

Jeff Carr has another suggestion. "Think of being more efficient. Learn to leverage knowledge and process. For example, coordinate and automate all responses from Frequently Asked Questions (FAQs). There is no need to reinvent the wheel for answers or options to questions clients commonly and frequently ask."

Lucy Endel Bassli, who served as assistant general counsel, legal operations at Microsoft for over thirteen years and is the author of the new book, *The Simple Guide to Legal Innovation*, suggests optimizing your use of technology. She says, "If you are generally comfortable with technology, then schedule time to become very comfortable with it in your professional life. Learn new ways of sharing your information and engaging clients. Everyday work is now different than expected, and technology certainly plays a big and likely lasting role."

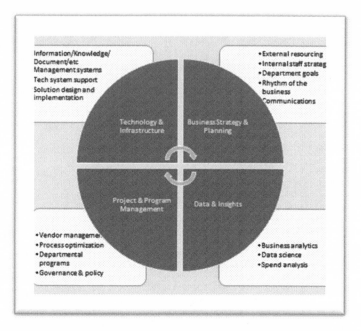

In her book, Lucy provides the simple breakdown, above, of the most critical legal operations functions that every legal department is either already exploring now or is contemplating the need for these various skillsets.

Create an innovation plan and/or program

Major accounting firms, like KPMG, Deloitte, and PwC, have been innovating for years, largely due to the more disciplined, top-down hierarchy they operate under. Most other professional services firm operate under a much more diffuse, decentralized, and horizontal hierarchy, where every equity partner has roughly equal say and decision-making power. As a result, many adapt, innovate, and change at a glacial rate.

Before 2020, at least two major law firms created formal innovation centers, such as Allen & Overy and Orrick, positioning themselves as one of the few major law firms who put a stake in the ground to establish the firm as "early adopters" committed to innovative solutions.

Formally review and assess all MBDCS investments

> To survive and thrive, all lawyers, firms, and other professionals must continue to invest in strategic marketing, selling, and related communications. Few firms or individual professionals without an effective marketing and sales program ever survive economic disruptions.
>
> – Ralph Baxter

Remember, every professional and business decision or choice you make has a direct impact on business development (as defined in Chapter 7) to one degree or another. The key during economic downturns is to continue to invest in MBDCS, but to do so more strategically. Even in booming economies, there are always efficiencies to be had in many MBDCS investments and projects.

As described in Chapter 9 of this book, conducting strategic assessments and reviews of the firm/practice, including all MBDCS investments, is critical to survival and growth during all economic conditions, but especially so after a pandemic, when the pressure on profitability intensifies.

For over thirty years, I have helped many firms and practitioners optimize their MBDCS programs and efforts. Over the years, I get similar requests: "How can we/I take our MBDCS program and efforts to the next level?"

Below are some best practices based on my experience. Ask yourself:

- ➢ "Is the firm's MBDCS program organized optimally in alignment with its go-to-market plan and strategies?" If not, consider whether reorganizing, restructuring, new hires, and/or reassigning roles and responsibilities would help increase ROI. (see Chapters 7 and 11)

- ➢ "What works best to measurably improve client service and results from MBDCS efforts?" If you do not have the metrics, information, or data to verifiably assess what works, now is the time to focus more on what can be measured. Using modern technology and business discipline, it is possible to measure ROI from most MBDCS efforts and programs.

- ➢ "Which MBDCS efforts account for the greatest amount of new business?" For example, requests for proposal/information/ qualifications (RFP/I/Q) account for an increasing percentage of annual revenues for many firms and providers. If so, a great strategic effort would be to improve your (RFP/I/Q) process and program.

- ➢ "What percentage of your annual work is done on a discounted basis, using a fixed or flat fee or another billing structure other than the billable hour (alternative fee arrangements, also known as AFAs)?" AFAs account for an increasing percentage of annual revenues for many firms and providers. Now is the time to formally assess, organize, and upgrade your billing strategy and process to include AFA options.

- ➢ "Does the firm's current support staff organizational structure dovetail with and coordinate all client-facing support functions in alignment with the go-to-market plan?" If not, consider combining all key business development, client-touching support departments to increase efficiencies in deliverables, coordination, and collaboration.

➤ "What are the most mission-critical investments to make or continue to make right now?" If you do not yet have a simple, strategic growth plan for your practice, firm, or department, now is the time to create one (see Chapter 11).

➤ "What can be eliminated, delayed, reused, improved, leveraged, etc.?" If a tool or type of MBDCS investment is not working or it is not possible to calculate an ROI, either stop doing it or do it much more strategically/selectively during economic downturns.

Step up your organic growth programs and efforts

It is well established that it takes much more time, money, and effort to get a brand-new client in the door than it does to get more work from an existing client, where a relationship of trust is already established.[54]

Yet, for a variety of reasons, many lawyers and other professional services providers who work in a firm setting struggle to effectively cross-sell or cross-service (defined as expanding the type or amount of work done for any individual client).[55]

In fact, Michael Rynowecer, President of BTI Consulting (https://bticonsulting.com/), says, "BTI research reveals the typical law firm has *only* 23% of a client's work available to them," and "clients often wonder why law firms and lawyers don't spend more time and effort trying to get more of their business."

Organic growth is defined as additional income received from existing clients, accounts, or markets, or from brand-new clients and markets. But, to date, most law firms and many other professional services firms have relied mainly on top-down, management-led acquisition and consolidation growth strategies, where they create and implement (often well-organized and funded) programs, strategies, and tactics designed to identify appropriate laterals to hire, other firms to absorb, or potential merger partners. This top-down, management-led growth has vastly increased the average size and scope of accounting firms, consulting firms, and AmLaw 200 law firms.

Yet, organic revenues and growth strategies are often the most profitable. But to be effective, they require buy-in and effort from all or most fee-earners in the firm, not just those serving in firm management roles.

Common obstacles to implementing effective organic growth programs within many professional services firms include:

- The current size and scale of most major firms allows fee-earners very little extra time to devote to proactive, organic growth initiatives.

- Billable-hour, non-billable hour, and work-life time demands.

- Credit issues, including origination, willingness to share, fiefdoms, hoarding, and which partner "owns" the relationship.

- The natural introversion of most highly educated professionals (as detailed in Chapter 4), which causes significant skepticism, desire to work and operate autonomously and independently, and resistance to adaptation or change.

Some leading firms have been able to overcome these common obstacles and have created and implemented successful, organized, organic growth programs—each involving the right mix of people, processes, and technology. What are some proven organic growth strategies and tactics being used by some professional services firms?

1. **Create or Upgrade Your Key Client Program**: If you do not yet have one, now is the time to create and implement one. If you already have a key client program operating, now is the time to formally review and assess it to determine what can and should be done to refresh and enhance it, so you stand out from competitors. Supercharge key client-account management programs by putting written key account annual plans on blast, by reconfiguring the staff support dedicated to key accounts, or by expanding hires (see below). Some firms are expanding their key account programs to

include clients who are not necessarily the largest clients of the firm, but are clients who are growing, acquiring, consolidating, or are going through other phases in the business life cycle. This is being accomplished by including relevant questions in required annual plans and hiring qualified staff to support these organic growth initiatives (see below).

2. **Putting Annual Plans on Blast:** For years, most firms have required that every firm partner, fee-earner, practice group, or department write an annual business or business development plan. Yet, in most firms, these plans sit on a shelf and are rarely used and rarely referred to, except around compensation time. Now, with the increased size and scale of many leading firms, these plans are increasingly being automated, tied to appropriate customer relationship management (CRM) programs (for example, SalesForce and OnePlace), experience databases (Intapp), or other AI or tracking technologies (sometimes as simple as Excel).

   All these programs are supported by firm staff members, whose job is to help fee-earners, teams, and groups accomplish the actions listed in their development plans and to regularly report efforts and results to firm leaders. This is one example of the effective use of people, processes, and technology to create and implement a strategic, results-oriented organic growth program.

   Other firms are successfully enhancing fee-earner and practice area/business unit accountability by coordinating plans, efforts, and communications that are critical to success. Many professional services firms now have a formal and successful Annual Planning process in place at the individual fee-earner level, which automatically (through the effective use of technology) dovetails into Practice Group/Area planning and/or Key Client Programs (or vice versa). Effective planning programs require a minimum of a mid-year review with key leadership (many firms use a quarterly review process) and are an efficient way to track and report efforts.

If well done, coordinated plans are executed in a much more efficient, measurable, and streamlined manner, allowing the firm to maximize the efforts of their greatest assets—their fee-earners. Firms that have an effective Annual Planning process in place, can point to a ten to thirty percent return on investment and many non-measurable, intangible benefits (especially more efficient uses of attorney time).

3. **Faster Formalization of Industry/Niche Groups and Teams:** The accelerated rate at which information flows has dramatically reduced the average business life cycle, i.e., the amount of time it takes for companies to be created, grow, consolidate, and die. In response, many firms are much quicker to identify trends and internally coordinate the fee-earners and staff with the experience to serve the industries or businesses involved. Having a deep industry focus and an accompanying, well-planned, and executed go-to-market strategy has proven to be effective for many leading firms and practitioners.[56]

Recent examples include firms creating organized, cross-functional teams to meet, market to, respond to, and serve clients during the 2020 crisis, in the cannabis industry, and those involved in the opioid and vaping crises, among others. How are these new and developing needs being identified and captured? By including relevant questions in required annual plans, such as, "What trends are you seeing in your practice?" or "Please list any new or novel problems, challenges, issues, technologies, or types of businesses you have been asked about, helped with, counseled on, or represented this past year and would like to do more of."

4. **Strategically Expanding Staff Support:** To organize, drive, and support the strategies described above and other related support needs, many leading firms have hired or are hiring different types of experienced executives and specialists. Examples include:

- **New C-Suite Positions** — New kinds of C-suite executives and director-level positions include value officers, client experience/service officers, pricing directors and officers, process management directors and officers, and practice management or operations directors and officers for the firm or individual groups.

- **More Business Development (BD) Specialists** – Many firms and CMBDOs are hiring BD specialists to provide the dedicated, needed support for client/account teams and industry/niche groups. Most BD specialist roles are primarily focused on doing the massive amounts of work needed to enable business development by generating new business opportunities using mainly seminars, events, sponsorships, writing, and speaking. Because most BD Specialists also have these other significant responsibilities, most lack the time to fully devote to sales, lead generation, and client development (which is, in and of itself, a full-time job).

- **Seasoned BD/Sales/Client Development Executives** – Compared with BD specialists, BD executive positions are much more client and potential-client facing on a day-to-day basis. These executive-level roles are being filled by professionals who have an executive presence; a deep and rich network; and have significant experience in successful client development and service with professional services firms.

Other than people, time and money are the most critical assets for all firms and practitioners, and time needs to be consistently tracked firmwide to improve productivity and profitability

For firms operating under a billable hour model, an important issue (and metric) is how the use of time impacts productivity and profitability. All fee-earners in billable hour firms keep their time, which drives all revenues and profitability. Yet, most professional staff members who support the fee-earners are not required to, nor do they keep their time. This is a mistake because productivity and ROI can only be meaningfully tracked and measured by knowing both the time and money spent for each project, but also on an annual basis. This is especially true for all MBDCS investments (staff and operating expenses), for which ROI can be challenging to quantify.

Most firms only track and evaluate the productivity of MBDCS staff informally by the number of tasks, projects or initiatives completed. This commonly used, informal tracking and reporting method does not provide the data and metrics needed to measure the two most important factor – how time and money are spent. Especially in firms with over 25 fee earners and associated staff. The only way to meaningfully track and benchmark productivity is to require time tracking by most (or all) firm employees. So, firms may want to consider having all business professionals employed by the firm to keep their time in the firm's time and billing system. The most successful chief MBDCS officers set up their teams timekeeping format to input time in 15-minute increments by person who made the request, practice/department/group, budget to be used, and project name, and regularly review and assess the use of time to maximize productivity.

For individual practitioners wanting to increase organic growth, the best strategy and approach is to ask clients, using questions like "What other problems, issues or challenges are you facing right now?", "What's coming up that you are concerned with?", etc. Or, create a survey method to regularly gather relevant information in a valid and usable manner by conducting a formal client survey or implementing a survey at the conclusion of each client engagement. There are numerous resources to help create and implement client surveys, both online and through experienced consultants.

Be careful when looking to fully automate client surveys, because, in the past, some of the best clients of some leading firms received a request to complete a survey after every single matter or case was concluded, which resulted in the best client(s) receiving dozens of emails to complete the survey each month. Obviously, this backfired on the firm's attempts to enhance and improve its relationships with clients.

Below is an example of the types of questions that can be asked in writing or verbally. The most important step of any client survey is to gather and track all responses in an organized and usable way, and to act upon them. Once acted upon, be sure to communicate any upgrades or changes that were made because of the clients' feedback on the surveys.

Client Experience & Satisfaction Criteria	Rating (Scale 1-10, with 10 highest)
Clearly communicates options, expectations, fees and costs before starting work	
Initiates and provides regular updates throughout representation/engagement	
Quickly responds to questions and requests	
Provides enough information to make you feel knowledgeable and prepared	
Schedules calls and meetings when convenient for you	
Responds quickly to my/our communications and requests	
All professionals and staff you worked with were professional, courteous and friendly	
Initiates periodic, unpromoted, proactive communications	
Provides value for the amount charged for the results and service delivered	
Easy to do business with	
Makes you feel your business is valued	

Organic growth strategies are the least risky to implement, and they are proven to strengthen a firm's profitability, market position, and competitive advantages. Yet too few professional services firms have strategic and effective organic growth programs in place, so consider which of the above options might help increase growth.

Enhance lateral acquisition, onboarding, and integration programs and efforts

Too many professional services firms separate the MBDCS functions and departments from the lateral hiring or departments. It is a strategic mistake that they are not operating and communicating in a coordinated and collaborative manner, because lateral hiring/acquisitions and MBDCS are the two largest drivers and producers of new revenues and clients (other than fee-earners).

A small handful of forward-thinking professional services firms have restructured and reorganized all the firm's administrative support departments to combine every single support department that "touches" the client under one new umbrella: billing, collections, MBDCS functions and lateral/hiring functions all fall under this new umbrella. See this article for more complete information:

www.lawjournalnewsletters.com/2018/10/01/chief-client-service-experience-and-value-officers-in-law-firms/.

For tips and ways to enhance and upgrade lateral hiring integration and retention efforts, see this article: www.lawfuel.com/blog/lateral-hires/.

Upgrade your requests for proposal/information/qualifications (RFP/I/Q) process

Below are four key things every firm and practitioners can do to be more competitive, win more work from proposals and RFP/I/Qs and make the best use of limited available time:

1. **How well do you and the practitioners in your firm evaluate the opportunity before deciding to respond to RFP/I/Q or develop a pitch?**

    Create and use an automated "go/no-go checklist" for practitioners to review and use (with or without the assistance of in-house MBDCS staff) to evaluate key strategic issues before spending a lot of non-billable time and resources responding to an RFP/I/Q or making a pitch.

    Below are a few key questions to include:

    - Are there any explicit or potential legal or business conflicts of interest?

    - Is this opportunity aligned with our firm or practice group strategy?

    - Can we offer strong competitive advantages?

    - Is the work a core competency of ours? Is it in our "sweet spot," i.e., what we excel at doing?

    - Can we get the desired result (the win) for the client?

- Will winning provide us with any competitive advantages?

- Can we staff and handle this work profitably? Can we offer data-informed pricing options?

- Do we know and can we contact the decision makers and influencers?

- Do we know the issuer's main reason for sending an RFP/I/Q (e.g., to save on costs, to improve quality, to enhance results)?

- Has the issuer or prospect already made a decision? Do the decision makers or influencers already favor an incumbent or competitor?

- What are the main selection factors or criteria? Will cost be a major factor in selecting the winning bid?

If your firm does not have automated systems to manage pricing, RFP/I/Q, proposals and responses, or if firm leadership does not encourage that all practitioners formally ask themselves specific questions (like the above) before deciding whether to respond or compete, consider addressing these two crucial issues.

2. **Does a designated key partner or firm representative personally contact the RFP/I/Q issuer, decision maker(s), and/or influencer(s) as appropriate *before* submitting a written response or pitching? And, while doing so take notes and communicate the response(s) internally, as appropriate?**

Numerous studies show that the chances of winning work fall exponentially when the respondents do not engage in some form of personal contact with the issuer, decision makers and/or influencers before or while drafting and submitting an RFP/I/Q response or developing a pitch.

Yet most practitioners do not engage in personal pre-contact by initiating a preliminary, introductory, appreciative phone call or sending appropriate emails before responding or pitching. Firms in the U.K. and Australia have significantly higher RFP/I/Q win rates than U.S.-based firms, mainly because they are trained to pre-contact for almost every RFP/I/Q or pitch opportunity.

Listed above are several questions to ask and issues to raise during the pre-contact call or email or (preferably) during an in-person, non-billable visit. Discussing these and other questions before the pitch will greatly increase a firm's chance to win the representation, work, engagement, case, or deal.

3. **Do you/does your firm have and use a formal post-RFP/I/Q pitch protocol? And, it is supported by firm leadership and are all fee-earners expected to utilize it?**

    Worldwide, less than half of firms have and use an established post-RFP or post-pitch evaluation process or checklist. Yet without such a process or checklist that is used consistently, it is impossible to know how best to use your limited time and resources to improve your win rate.

    Effective post-RFP/I/Q and post-pitch protocols often include a centralized method for contacting the issuer and/or relevant decision makers; a qualified person to make the contact, call, or visit; a list of key and common debriefing or after-action questions; copious notes and tracking of the response; and analyzing and using the information to improve.

4. **Does your firm annually and formally identify and track which of its key, existing clients and best prospects issue and use RFP/I/Q to retain outside practitioners?**

    If not, your firm will remain in a *reactive* posture, i.e., only responding to RFP/I/Qs once the request arrives at the firm. If this is the case at your firm, consider hiring a client service/relations specialist to proactively gather this information and to work to be sure your firm is on all short lists for all key clients' and prospects' panel reviews, major and one-off engagements, litigations and transactions, and other competitive bids.

Remember, overall, business development itself is a process (as defined in Chapter 7), and many commonly used MBDCS tools also follow a process to get planned, implemented, completed, and followed up upon. So, a blog and a webinar alone will not necessarily be effective at generating an ROI. Sustainable investments of money, time, and effort must be made strategically and over time, to yield measurable results.

Upgrade how you monitor companies, organizations, industries, and sectors and stay in touch and communicate with key clients, referral sources, and contacts

1. Know the Lay of the Land: If you practice in a firm setting, no client or client contact is 100% yours alone. If you are an associate, counsel, or a non-equity partner, you are usually one lawyer or fee-earner (of several or many) working for the partner in charge of the client relationship (the originating partner). There are often other fee-earners within your firm who also know and work with these and similar client contacts.

So, it's of primary and foremost importance to keep your INTERNAL clients (usually the firm's primary relationship partner and/or other fee-earners who work for the EXTERNAL client) informed ahead of time about what you plan to do, plan to communicate, want to do, and may learn/discover from your efforts/communications with your client contacts.

The same applies to the other professional services providers who work with and for your key clients. For example, if you do not know who does their accounting, data security, etc. work to find out so that you can meet and establish relationships with the client's other outside professional services providers as appropriate.

2. Connect Online to All Key Client/Contacts and "Follow" Their Organization's Page: Send a tailored request to connect with each key client/contact on LinkedIn. Make sure to "follow" them and their organization/company's LinkedIn and Twitter pages.

3. Create Auto-Alerts from Key Online Sources and Subscribe to Relevant RSS feeds/Blogs of Key Clients and for Key Industries/Issues:

Ask your firm's Library or MBDCS staff members what is available to you at your firm and how to access, sign up or subscribe.

4. Meet with the Firm's Primary Relationship Partner for the Client: Request a time to meet with them, take him/her to lunch, or take coffee to his/her office to have a dedicated conversation about each key client/contact as relevant/appropriate. Remember, their time is valuable and in demand, so think about bringing the Partner some useful information you have uncovered and that the Partner may not already know about this client(s).

Ask what else you can do to stay abreast of the client's business, industry, trends. Come armed with some suggestions, take notes. Do and deliver what is suggested, and keep the partner updated, either personally or through regular global updates the partner can distribute to the team of fee-earners and professional support staff who serve the client.

If appropriate, volunteer to work in a fully dedicated manner for one client only for a day each week or month, or on a specific matter or case for a certain period of time. Offer to do so remotely or, as possible, offer to work on-site at the client's office during that time.

Similarly, discuss with your group or department leader whether a remote or on-site (as is possible) "secondment" for a specific period for any client might be a win/win for the client and firm. Continually explore with the partner what else you can do to help you maintain, secure, and develop the firm's relationship with each client.

5. Review Your Firm's Email Distribution List(s): (which are often maintained in your firm's MBDCS Department). If your clients are already on the firm's email distribution lists and are being sent relevant electronic communications from the firm (for which they have opted-in), such as advisories and invitations to firm events, make sure your firm's MBDCS representatives inform you when they accept, so you can be sure to attend, too. If your list of key clients and contacts and all your LinkedIn connections are not yet on the firm's distribution lists, please schedule a meeting with your MBDCS representatives to invite them to opt-in as appropriate.

See Appendix 1 and 2 for many more options, tips, and suggestions.

The critical role of utilizing a Client Relationship Management (CRM) system

As described in Chapter 7, one of the most important yet glaring issues within most professional services firms is that not all client contacts, prospective client contacts, referral sources, vendors, and LinkedIn connections are housed in one single platform, i.e., there is no single master list of all people known by all firm members, professional staff, and employees. Nor are all or most MBDCS communications and outreaches tracked in one place.

Why is this such a glaring issue and mistake? Because people are the most valuable and important asset of every professional services firm and practitioner, yet not being able to access them in an efficient way and through a single source causes a host of issues that can have a negative impact on the firm's and fee-earners' reputations. How? By engaging in overlapping and redundant communications.

For example, over the years many C-suite executives have told me they are often called by several partners from the same firm within a week or so, all asking essentially the same question: "Can I have some work?" Not only is this distasteful from the client's perspective, it also tarnishes the firm's image by showing how uncoordinated the firm's systems and communications are. Many clients are annoyed by these types of redundant and overlapping communications and consider them as less than professional.

Leading accounting and consulting firms that require all practitioners to opt-in all their contacts into the firm's CRM system avoid this embarrassment, and it gives them a major competitive advantage, because it allows them to be thorough, efficient, targeted, and professional with all work, service, MBDCS, and other outreach. Rarely do the firms with mandatory opt-in and fully integrated CRM systems embarrass themselves with redundant, overlapping, and repetitive communications to clients, prospects, and other contacts, as often happens to firms without a fully integrated CRM system.

There are many CRM platforms available in the market, but it is important to not only procure and implement one that will also work with relevant data from other key sources (such as conflicts, time, and billing, etc.; Intapp (www.intapp.com) is one solution that does this), but to also upgrade firm policies about contact intake and automatic opt-in. Plus, firm leaders should provide direction, guidance, and how tos, and allocate non-billable time for each fee-earner to routinely review, clean, and update their contact list.

Lavinia Calvert, who serves as General Manager, Marketing & Business Development Business at Intapp, said, "One client recently challenged his business development team, asking what it would normally take to prepare a partner for meeting a key-client. They came back with fourteen steps involving multiple systems and sources of data to prepare a holistic view of the client relationship. He brought that challenge to us. Our platform integrates answers to most of those steps in one place. (She is referring to Intapp's OnePlace for Marketing platform[57]). That is the benefit of a platform designed to serve the unique needs of professional services firms. Data can be connected, normalized, and centralized across the entire client lifecycle."

In fact, increasing the use of data to enhance client relationships is an opportunity, because few firms provide clients with a data-driven look at what they do for them, yet clients want data and other relevant information. (See chart below.)

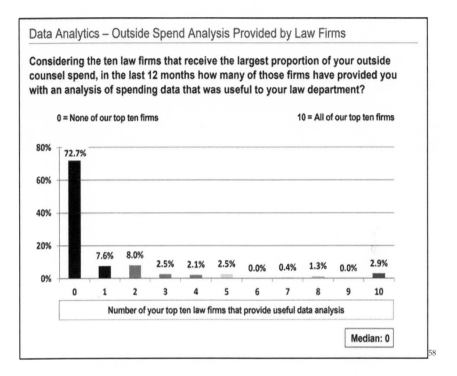

Data Analytics – Outside Spend Analysis Provided by Law Firms

Considering the ten law firms that receive the largest proportion of your outside counsel spend, in the last 12 months how many of those firms have provided you with an analysis of spending data that was useful to your law department?

0 = None of our top ten firms   10 = All of our top ten firms

Number of your top ten law firms that provide useful data analysis

Median: 0

Consider expanding or creating strategic partnerships to enhance corporate citizenship

People everywhere want to work for organizations whose missions resonate with them intellectually and emotionally.[59]

The need for pro bono legal advice surged during the 2020 crisis. The leaders at Suffolk University Law School, based in Boston, Massachusetts, realized this early on in the crisis and, as a result, the school's Legal Innovation & Technology Lab immediately took action, in cooperation with the Massachusetts Access to Justice Commission's CV19 Task Force, to plan a response that would help fill the gap.

Together, using an open-source document assembly platform and other collaboration tools, they designed, created, and implemented (pro bono) the Document Assembly Line Project (a pandemic response) (https://suffolklitlab.org/doc-assembly-line). It creates and provides mobile-friendly online court forms and pro se materials for the state of Massachusetts for key areas of urgent legal need amidst the crisis.

Gabriel H. Teninbaum, a leading innovation and technology expert in the legal sector and professor at the Suffolk University Law School, who is also the Director, Institute on Legal Innovation & Technology, Co-Director, Legal Innovation & Technology Concentration, and Director, Legal Innovation & Technology Certificate Program, says, "We also shared our work and code online, in the hopes it can be replicated in other jurisdictions."

Every firm should review its Social Impact and Sustainability Program to ensure its appropriateness in this new environment. Is the firm utilizing its highest and best skills to help address the challenges facing society, post-pandemic? "Now is the time for each firm to leverage its unique skills and relationships to collaborate with clients and third-parties toward an improved future-state," said Pamela Cone, Founder and CEO of Amity Advisory (www.amityadvisory.com), a social-impact consultancy for the legal industry.

This process includes a review of past initiatives to determine which could be made more sustainable. Think beyond an isolated effort or transaction. Instead, think about how to enhance, improve, or expand the efforts you have done or been involved with in the past, to increase your reputation for corporate responsibility.

"It is no longer sufficient to engage in 'random acts of kindness.' Rather, society is expecting the professions to lead the way with meaningful, transformational initiatives—beyond the charitable or pro bono efforts you have done in the past. Successful social-impact programs must be strategic: core to the business, consistent with purpose, and collaborative in nature," Pam continued. "The firms that understand and move quickly will emerge as leaders in the eyes of clients and recruits."

Increase your commitment to client value

Client value is the total benefit that you and your firm provide throughout the course of the business relationship, including tangible and intangible deliverables. Client value is experienced and defined by the client, not the lawyer or other service provider. If you are *assuming* or think that you already know everything about what your client(s) value, and are also *assuming* that all fee-earners and professional staff are consistently delivering value to clients, now is the time to conduct a formal client survey and/or create a client value map.

Remember, all clients want: quality, cost-effective solutions; direct, straightforward, easy-to-digest, and practical business advice and guidance they can take to business leadership; a diverse team that initiates, suggests, and brings a wide range of solutions and options (as appropriate); innovative technology options, and unprompted outreach to educate and warn about developing, upcoming or potential risks.

If your firm does not yet have a proven, client-facing chief client value officer or the equivalent, now is the time to consider hiring one on a permanent, contract, or temporary basis. Several are experienced yet non-traditional rainmakers who communicate with major clients and referral sources regularly. Many know the business development process well and are trained in how to sell solutions (not just technical practices). This article describes how some leading firms are using dedicated chief value officers or the equivalent in major law firms:

http://www.lawjournalnewsletters.com/2018/10/01/chief-client-service-experience-and-value-officers-in-law-firms.

Build in and schedule time to plan ahead to be prepared for inevitable economic downturns

One practical (yet not easy to make time for) survival tactic is to schedule and regularly make time to stop, reflect, and think to yourself, "What's developing? What's probable? What's possible?" and then act upon those thoughts. Don't just think about these questions then permit yourself to get distracted and let those thoughts go.

Instead, consider calling a meeting to brainstorm ideas, possible solutions, technologies, strategies, and options relevant to your practice, industry, or sector. Invite a small group of the smartest, most experienced, or innovative thinkers, experts, and influencers you currently know and work with, along with others whom you may not know who work in your professional, industry or sector, to add a fresh perspective.

This is precisely what Kirk Sanderson did in early-2018, during a time when the global economy and his bread-and-butter business, mergers and acquisitions (M&A) and other transactions, were booming (along with the rest of the economy).

Kirk clearly understood that deal flow was cyclical, but he had the foresight to know his business should begin preparing during the best of times. So, he thought to himself, "When the M&A decides to take a turn, what else can we do to continue to bring value to our markets?"

Kirk acted upon this thought. He organized a brainstorming session in early-2018, which generated the idea for and ultimately resulted in a new and award-nominated technology he launched in late 2019, ContractsCompare (CC) (www.contractscompare.com; previously known as the M&A EasyReader). CC was inspired by and the result of the day-to-day challenges Kirk experienced with standard document comparison tools he used for his M&A business.

"Over the years, I had had multiple discussions with my relationships in the legal field that struggle with the same issue and couldn't find anyone that knew of an existing solution–so I decided to go out and build one," said Kirk.

CC was one of five finalists in the *Product Innovation Competition* held at AmLaw Media's *Legalweek* conference in February 2020. (CC was nominated under its previous name, M&A Easy Reader.)

CC saves parties significant time when negotiating and finalizing contracts and other agreements. It allows users to compare multiple subsequent versions of a single negotiated agreement in an easy-to-use dashboard that eliminates the need to endlessly scroll to find pertinent definitions and referenced sections, and it tracks changes and redlines to tell the story of negotiations as they evolve over time. CC is built to work seamlessly with iManage and iDocs.

Increase your commitment to diversity and pro bono

Many large law firms have made major commitments to the Mansfield Rule or signed on to the Move the Needle fund (www.mtnfund2025.com) led and managed by Diversity Lab (www.diversitylab.com.) In addition, one major law firm has increased its commitment to and investment in diversity by hiring professional staff dedicated to working only with the firm's diverse lawyers to help build their skills and practice.

Another example is the work being done by Legal Metrics, which is a consortium of over sixty major law firms, legal departments, and leading general counsel. This consortium was assembled and is led by David Cunningham, who serves as Chief Information Officer, Winston & Strawn (www.winston.com). The Legal Metrics consortium is currently in the process of creating a legal industry-wide D&I Dashboard for firms and departments to use once done.

One leading global law company tracks and reports D&I information in an exemplary manner: Elevate (https://elevateservices.com). For those not familiar with Elevate, it's a highly regarded law company that provides consulting and technology services to law departments and law firms all over the world.

In late 2018, John Croft, president and co-founder of Elevate, spearheaded the effort to organize and produce the company's first-ever Equitability & Inclusion report that surveys, tracks, and publicly reports the company's diversity statistics of *all* Elevate's employees.[60] This is an example of inclusion at its best.[61]

Former Justice of the Michigan Supreme Court Kurtis T. Wilder currently serves as Of Counsel to Butzel Long, where he concentrates his practice in resolving disputes via negotiation and mediation, and in representing clients in complex litigation and appeals. Throughout his distinguished career, Justice Wilder has been an active supporter of many

civic, philanthropic, and pro bono endeavors and is a leader in supporting diversity in the legal profession.

Kurt says, "At all times, and especially during crises, it's our job as lawyers to use our unique skills to help all of our communities. Many lawyers and other legal professionals tend to forget that non-profits (and quasi-government organizations) are the third leg of the stool supporting our communities, together with government and business. Helping nonprofits and quasi-government organizations navigate difficult challenges creates goodwill and builds relationships and future opportunities."

There are many affinity groups dedicated to supporting and increasing D&I. One example is Mothers Esquire (www.mothersesquire.com/groups), whose mission is to achieve gender equity in the legal profession by improving promotion and retention rates of women in the law, along with championing equal pay and transparency regarding compensation practices in the legal profession. Consider increasing your support of and participation in these and other relevant D&I groups and efforts.

Also consider enhancing the metrics used to measure and calculate ROT from D&I investments, programs, and initiatives.[62]

Strategic options for financially strong firms and practices

- **Strategic acquisitions:** An obvious opportunity to leverage and grow during any economic downturn is through acquisitions. If competing firms are closing, companies are divesting and selling assets, and banks are foreclosing, there is opportunity. The key is to stay in contact with select competitors, bankers, and other service providers and to follow appropriate news feeds.
- **Creating and launching strategic new services or products:** If possible, consider creating and unveiling new products or services that clients need now or related to the firm's specialties. Doing so will help diversify income and help the firm stand out from the competition.
- **Strategically retaining or hiring new talent:** The immediate reaction to any economic downturn is to tighten your belt. But we know that great professional talent (people) are a key to success and to surviving and thriving. So, depending on your strategic objectives and choices, identify the gaps where experienced talent could add value and make measurable contributions.
- **Strategic diversification:** Major accounting and consulting firms have had consulting arms for decades. Prior to the 2020 crisis, some major law firms like Epstein Becker & Green, (www.ebgadvisors.com) and McDermott Will & Emery, (www.mcdermottplus.com) launched subsidiaries or consulting arms focused on health care regulatory issues, such as insurance reimbursement of Medicare, Medicaid, and Affordable Care Act costs.

Other major law firms created new subsidiaries focused on nonlegal issues, such as[63]:

- Bryan Cave Leighton Paisner's BCLP Cubed (www.bclplaw.com), providing high-volume work and legal operations consulting.

- Wilson Sonsini's legal automation platform, SixFifty (www.sixfifty.com).

- Eversheds Sutherland's legal consulting and staffing firm, Konexo (www.eversheds-sutherland.com).

- Greenberg Traurig's shared solutions platform, Recurve.[64]

If a diversification strategy can develop new revenues or clients and/or better serve clients in your main practice areas/industries or niches, now is the time to consider relevant diversification options. But do so methodically, because most diversification efforts take considerable investments of time, money, and effort, over time to become profitable.

This chapter does not necessarily include every strategic option or choice. Many others are described in previous chapters in this book. This chapter highlights some of the strategic choices that have proven to be most critical, profitable, and successful for others.

Once you have made your key strategic decisions and choices, it is time to convert them into a simple, yet actionable plan so that you can be sure they meet or exceed their desired goals and ROI.

Key Takeaways

> Pandemics will reoccur, so always be prepared to pivot and fast.
> The main goal should (always) be to enhance your relationships with key people and stakeholders.
> To deliver measurable results, all strategic choices and decisions for professional services involve or need:
  o Clients and key stakeholders' input and feedback in a valid, usable format.
  o Careful planning, including impact and prioritization considerations.
  o An optimal combination of people/staff, processes/ procedures, and technology.
  o Taking risk(s), the level of which varies considerably depending on many factors.

11

DRAFT & IMPLEMENT A SIMPLE ACTION PLAN

> Once the fog lifts from the corona virus crisis, every professional needs to dust themself off and work to understand and embrace the inevitable changes in the way business will be conducted from now on.
>
> – Ralph Baxter

The key to attaining real and measurable results from any strategic choice is to make it actionable, and to hold yourself accountable. Due to time demands, many firms and professional services providers only *talk* about strategy and strategic choices they would like, are thinking about, or plan to implement. As the saying goes, "talk is cheap." To make sure you act upon and implement your strategic choices; many studies show that you need to put your goals and strategic choices in writing[65] in an actionable manner.

Why does putting goals and strategic choices in WRITING apply especially to professional services firms and providers? As we all know, time is one of the most valuable, precious, and limited commodities. For most professional services providers, because they work under a billable-time model, there is very little "extra" time available to do all the necessary, important, but not necessarily urgent things needed to build and develop a practice (see Chapter 6). Due to billable hour requirements and other demands on their available time, it's very difficult for most busy professional service providers to be proactive, carve out time to be proactive, or to make time for MBDCS or to upgrade client service efforts.

As described in Chapter 6, consider using false deadlines to create forced efficiency upon yourself and your team.[66] The law of forced efficiency says: "There is never enough time to do everything, but there is always enough time to do the most important thing."

If you already have a firmwide, department, practice area/group, or individual strategic business plan in writing, now is the time to review and update it to adapt to the fundamental changes already caused and the new changes that will likely be caused by the 2020 pandemic. Do not do this alone based only on your own thoughts and perspective. Instead, work in groups, ask trusted colleagues, mentors, and others, or invite input from an experienced, independent professional.

What does a simple strategic business plan look like? Taking information contained in this book, here is an example:

- Identify a working team dedicated to strategic business planning for the firm or my practice, whether myself (for some of the below) only, existing colleagues and staff members, or consider using other experienced assistance virtually. Schedule and hold a virtual strategic business planning meeting. Appoint a scribe who will put all discussion notes, ideas, and decisions in writing, and maintain, update and report on it over time. Make assignments of who will do what regarding each of the below.

- Mark deadlines: one month from today, schedule the actual deadline, and also one week prior to whatever the actual deadline is, to remind you to do this (i.e., false deadlines).

- Conduct interviews with my top five clients and referral sources (both internal and external), and my top five past clients, asking similar questions and tracking all response in writing (Word, Excel, or another automated program), and gather all other client feedback from every other source and program. Compile and analyze to make adjustments.

- Update key metrics, such as expected billed and collected hours, work and opportunity pipeline, budget, and profitability projections.

- Review and assess physical office space needs, current lease, and adjustments that should or need to be made.

- Review my current marketing, business development, client development, and client service processes (MBDCS), and select the most appropriate and proven and effective MBDCS strategies, tools, and tactics.

- Consider mapping my client service/experience/journey process to consider implementing upgrades or making adjustments.

- Identify and sign up for a well-regarded unconscious-bias training program and pro bono efforts to get involved in.

- From the above, create an actionable to-do list with my team, and schedule deadlines and check-in meetings.

Here is an example of a simple Excel template that can be created and used for a strategic business or action plan (SAP). It is possible to have the "person responsible" and "due date" cells tied to Outlook so a summary or reminder automatically pops up in your Outlook (but a technology expert is usually needed to program the Excel spreadsheet and cells to do this).

Once drafted, commit to reviewing and adjusting your SAP as things change and develop or once a month, then create automated reminders in your calendar to make sure you do so. Lucy Endel Bassli, author of *The Simple Guide to Legal Innovation*, says, "We know all the sayings about how plans are made, and then life happens. Accept that the best-laid business plan may need adaption and modification. Flexibility will need to come in several aspects: who you take on as clients, the kind of work you do, and how you get the work done."

Strategic Business Plan

Strategic Choice	Person Responsible	To-Dos	Due Date

In the years leading up to the 2020 crisis, many professional services firms invested significant amounts of time, money, and effort into brainstorming and creating formal SAPs. Yet, too often, once done, they are rarely reviewed, tracked, or used. So, whether the goals and objectives have been attained or even completed are often not measured or known for certain.

If you do not have an existing strategic business plan in writing, now is the time to create one. It does not need to be lengthy or complex, but it needs to be communicated to all stakeholders and used, reviewed, updated, and acted upon regularly.

The same applies to annual business plans required by firm leadership to create or fill out an annual business or business development plan. Yet, once done, due to time demands, most professional services providers simply ignore their plan and rarely refer to it or use it (except at year-end or before compensation time). Instead, they should consider using their annual plan as a guidepost throughout the year, to be sure they implement what they planned.

To do so, attach your SAP to your calendar and schedule. For example, create a recurring weekly or monthly calendar meeting or appointment with yourself. Name it something like "SAP/Marketing/BusDev Follow-Up," attach your annual plan to the calendar meeting, and each time that meeting pops up, force yourself to devote at least five to thirty minutes to do *at least one thing* listed on your plan, whether it's as simple as making one phone call or sending one email to set up a lunch or meeting. If the meeting pops up and you are buried in something else so cannot take any time, move the meeting to a few days later, to remind you again. Then, discipline yourself to devote the time.

For example, my primary mission, goal, and objective (both in life and professionally) is to be viewed and thought about as a person/professional who adds value to one or to many in all my communications, behaviors, actions, and choices. I strive to be known as someone who makes everything a bit better, brighter, more successful, more fun, or useful because I was there or involved.

How does this translate into an SAP? I simply ask myself regularly (and before any call, email, or communication):

- "What can I say or do during this call, meeting, or in this email that will be helpful, useful, informative or of interest?"

- "What is or could be my greatest contribution/value add?"

- "What is my highest and best use?"

- "What is the most valuable use of my time right now?"

Because I have been implementing my strategic mission and plan for many years now, it is a habit, but I still create and use automated, self-imposed false deadlines and reminders, so I make sure to do what is most important, even if not urgent.

It's critical to adjust and adapt in the immediate aftermath of a crisis, to continue operating, practicing, and serving clients. But the need to formally plan and do so effectively, efficiently, and in the most useful, doable manner is never more important than it is after a pandemic.

Strategic business planning is a proven discipline that takes time and effort but yields considerable dividends when done well. As Benjamin Franklin, the father of time management, once said, "Failing to plan is planning to fail."

Remember, as Ralph Baxter said, "There will be no returning to the exact same 'normal' as we knew it before the 2020 crisis hit. Instead, a new reality will emerge. The key is to focus on the foundation of all professional services, and the fact that it is and will always be a human-centric business."

And as Jeff Carr says, "The days of being built on inefficiency are gone. Law firms and other professional services firms need to move quickly from a one-to-one to a one-to-many B2B (business-to-business) model."

Key Takeaways

> Failing to plan is planning to fail
> Plans do not need to be lengthy or complex, but they must be actionable.
> Tie the to-dos associated with your plan to your automated calendar (see Chapter 6 for more tips).
> To make the best use of your limited nonbillable time, ask for, obtain, or hire support and assistance as needed.

CONCLUSION

If you feel motivated after reading this book, remember that motivation is what may get you going or started, but *commitment* is what gets things done and delivers measurable results.

So, simply reading this guidebook, setting it aside, and eventually forgetting about it will not necessarily help you survive and thrive after a pandemic.

As mentioned on pages 9-10, in How to Get the Most Out of this Book, formally capturing the takeaways you gained from reading this book, those you think will be of most benefit to you, your firm, or practice, is critical to making them actionable and getting measurable results.

The content in this book most relevant to each firm or practitioner must also be tailored for each firm and practitioner, because each practice consists of numerous variables, such as type of practice, target markets, strengths, preferences, skills, knowledge, and other variants.

If you did not capture the content that most resonates for you as you read this book, you can set aside and schedule time now to review what you gleaned, to determine what may apply to your practice and routine. Remember that time and effort are required to get new or strategic goals accomplished in a measurable manner is usually considerable. Plus, simply thinking about or talking about what you want or plan to do will not get things done. You must make a *commitment*.

Several studies show that putting your goals in writing dramatically increases the chance you will accomplish them.[67] But simply putting them in writing is not enough, either. They must be acted upon, and most goals take consistent effort over time to accomplish.

Ideally, while or after reading this, you have identified, taken notes, or made a list of your key takeaways, action items, or other strategic things you want to do and implement in coming days, weeks, and months. Even better if you drafted a simple list or action plan as described in Chapter 11.

If you already have a simple, SAP in writing, congratulations!

Now, it's time to implement it. To make the best use of your valuable and limited time, and to allow you to focus on what you do best (practice your profession and serve your clients), enlist support and assistance to leverage your available time and to help you get the items in your SAP drafted, done, and implemented. This is critical, because all busy professionals have very little available non-billable or extra time (as described in Chapter 6).

Ways to enlist professional support for your SAP and get things done in a measurable manner

Most professionals have access to internal support from various staff, other business professionals, mentors, and departments. Review your SAP and decide who could help you get each strategic project or task accomplished, then reach out to them.

If you have not yet created an SAP in writing, enlist help by asking appropriate in-house business professionals for help (such as members of your firm's MBDCS, client service, or client value team, or if your firm has an internal business development coach, ask them).

If you do not have internal support available to leverage your time, or if the in-house professionals do not have the bandwidth to get done what you need, consider vetting and utilizing a qualified virtual assistant or external coach.

Be sure to use a professional who will not simply talk with you about what needs to be done or what you should do. Instead, make sure they will help you get things drafted, done, and implemented, so you can focus most of your time on what you do best: practicing your profession and delivering solutions to your clients.

For example, most strategic tasks and projects require something to be drafted, such as proposals, emails, talking points, checklists, blogs, and social media posts, etc. So, ask for help or hire a professional who will create drafts for you, which will save you considerable time. Make sure they will initiate a check-in or follow-up meeting schedule to be proactively accountable for what they create and do for you.

If you decide to retain an outside coach, be sure to introduce them to your in-house staff, including your assistant, MBDCS, client service or client value staff members, so the coach can work with them directly to coordinate and get things done for you, which again will save you considerable time and effort.

We all know that pandemics will occur again, the economy will continue to fluctuate, and other crises will happen. To survive and thrive, professional service providers need to be ready to adapt and change. The competitive pressure to be better, predictable, transparent, and more cost-effective, faster has never been greater.

This book allows you to regain a sense of certainty and control because it allows you to determine the next best steps to build your practice or firm in the wake of the pandemic and is a step-by-step guide to do just that.

Thank you for buying this book and helping support Global Giving, www.GlobalGiving.org!

If you liked this book, please consider:
- ❖ Writing and posting an honest book review on Amazon.
- ❖ Buying more copies of this book for your entire team or practice group on Amazon (or contact the author to obtain information about volume discounts: Julie@BusDevInc.com).
- ❖ Buying the other books I wrote on Amazon or from my website: https://busdevinc.com/books.html

If you'd like to do additional reading or check out any of the books and resources used in writing this book, a full bibliography is available here, on my website: https://busdevinc.com/books.html.

If you have any questions, comments, or would like to talk, please contact me, the author of this book, Julie Savarino:

Telephone: +1 (734) 276-1900

Email: Julie@BusDevInc.com

Website: www.BusDevInc.com.

SINCERE APPRECIATION AND ACKNOWLEDGMENTS

In my experience, nothing meaningful or worthwhile is ever accomplished alone. Without the support, assistance, and help I get every day from *so many* people and professionals, my life, career, and this book would never have been possible.

My parents, grandparents, siblings, aunts, uncles, cousins, in-laws, nieces, and nephews, friends, extended family, and my valued colleagues are what makes my life worth living. They advise, guide, and support me every day. Without them, I would be nothing, and this book would never have been written. To respect privacy, I am intentionally not listing them each by name. They know who they are. My heartfelt thanks and appreciation to each and every one of them and to God is infinite.

I also extend my sincere thanks to all my current and former clients, colleagues, and referral sources. I have had the honor and privilege of working for and with thousands of lawyers and other professional services providers, as well as hundreds of leading law firms, legal vendors and suppliers, networks, associations, and other professional services organizations and related entities, firms and companies (a partial list is available on my website, (www.busdevinc.com/clients_say.html).

The cumulative knowledge, skills, and experience I have gained by working with, knowing them and being of service to them is priceless.

I am good at many things, but I am not a professional author or book publisher. So, as I do for most of my projects, I assembled a virtual working team to advise me and help me get this book written, finished, and published. The team includes my amazing assistant, my talented freelance graphic designer, my external computer expert, all the experts I interviewed and quoted in this book, the advance copy readers, my incredible freelance proofreader, book editor, and formatter, and others.

I sincerely thank each of them for their patience, knowledge, insights, responsiveness, work ethic, and relentless commitment to help me get this book published. Again, to protect privacy, I am not listing their names, but if you would like me to refer you to them to help you with a future book or other projects, please contact me.

ABOUT THE AUTHOR

Julie Savarino is a leading expert in business and client development, and client experience, value, and service. During her thirty-year career, she has helped many law firms, lawyers, and other professional services firms and providers develop significant new business and measurably enhance client satisfaction and value. Julie is a top-100 thought leader on LinkedIn, holds a JD and MBA, and devotes pro bono time to support diversity, inclusion, veteran-related, charitable, and community causes. She currently serves as Chief Client Experience & Value Officer at Business Development Inc., https://busdevinc.com/

Email: Julie@BusDevInc.com
Phone: (734) 276-1900
LinkedIn: https://www.linkedin.com/in/juliesavarino/
Twitter: @JulieSavarino

APPENDIX 1

HOW TO DEFINE YOUR TARGET MARKET(S)

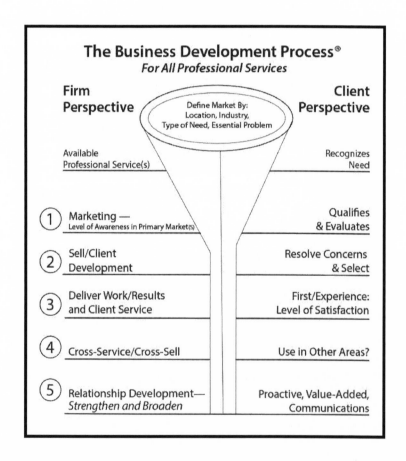

"Targets" are either a definable market(s) as a whole and/or a list of the select organizations and decision-makers within them that a fee-earner wants to secure or expand as meaningful and profitable client and/or referral relationships. To define your target market(s) and rank your opportunities, follow these steps:

1. **Create a list of targets/people that includes both external and internal resources in these categories:**

   A. **Current/existing clients:**

      i.   Key/primary/biggest ones, most recent and cumulative over time

      ii. Those with the potential to do more of the type of work you are already doing for them

      iii. Those with the potential to do other kinds of work (work that another practice group or partner does)

      iv. Past clients (those with whom you have a good relationship and who likely will need/can use additional services)

   B. **Prospective, brand-new clients**

   C. **Current/existing referral sources**

   D. **Potential referral sources**

Once you've completed step 1, go on to step 2, which is where you will assign appropriate target definitions to your top 10 best existing clients, prospects, and referral sources (both internal and external). Then, list the 3–5 highest-potential targets in each category above. Refer to the checklist at "3." (below) for help selecting your top 3–5.

2. **Define your key target markets/clients/prospects by whichever 2–3 of the items listed below best apply to each:**

   A. **Demographics** — What is their location, geographical footprint, industry, etc.?

    i. **Location** — Where are they located? What country, city, state, county, neighborhood?

    ii. **Size** — How big are your best clients/targets in terms of annual revenue and number of employees?

    iii. **Industry** — What's their specific field of business? If they manufacture something, what is it? If they provide services, what kind? What is the primary SIC classification for their business/field?

B. **Market share** — Are they a leader, runner-up, or distant follower in their market?

    i. **Socioeconomics** — What is their gender, age, income, occupation, education, stage in life cycle, interests, etc.?

    ii. **Type of Entity and/or Structure** — What is their xxxx?

    iii. **Corporate Structure** — Are they a corporation, LLC, LLP, PC, franchisor, franchisee, alliance, JV, spin-off, nonprofit, government entity or something else?

    iv. **Governance/Funding** — Are they VC backed, private equity owned, public, private, family owned, closely held?

    v. **Stage of Growth** — Are they start-up, emerging, pre-IPO, high growth, sustainable growth, maturing, declining?

C. **Type of Case/Issue/Problem and/or Circumstance**

    i. **Issue(s)** — What's the specific problem they need to have solved and how does that match what you or your firm is best able to solve?

    ii. **Type of Project/Transaction/Litigation**

    iii. **Transitions/Changes** — Are the experiencing or planning a RIF, acquisition, merger, sale, restructuring, IPO, going private, spin-off, management change, etc.?

    iv. **Compliance** — What do they have to get done in their business so as not to run afoul of local, state, and/or national legal or governmental requirements?

    v. **Aspirations** — What do they want to be different when the engagement is complete? Where do they see their company or industry or their own careers or economic circumstances in one to five years?

D. **Psychographics** — How would you describe their culture, attitudes, approach to business and legal issues, values, style, etc.?

    i. Does their corporate culture or industry culture match your firm?

    ii. Are they low budget and execution oriented or are they high end and strategy oriented? Combative or collaborative?

    iii. Staid or fashionable?

    iv. Degree of loyalty?

    v. Litigation philosophy/approach to litigation/outside counsel guidelines?

    vi. Level of professionalism and ethics in approach to business?

    vii. Other relevant factors?

3. **Checklist of items to consider when ranking your top 3–5 in each category as described in "1." above:**

A. **Revenue** — Clients that generate revenue in larger increments are preferable.

B. **Profit** — Clients that generate higher profit per engagement are preferable.

C. **Scale** — Clients that offer opportunity for larger engagements over time and consume service offerings that generate significant returns for the least amount of effort are preferable.

D. **Recurrence** — Clients that generate a consistent revenue stream over time are preferable.

E. **Professionalism** — Clients that behave professionally and are "easier" to work with are preferable.

F. **Accessibility** — Potential clients that are easy to identify, reach and communicate with are preferable.

G. **Skill Fit** — Potential clients whose demographics, socioeconomics, behavior, and circumstances closely match the fee-earners and/or firm's skill set are preferable.

H. **Aspirations** — With what kinds of clients do you and your colleagues desire and aspire to be working?

The next step is to consider the range of all possible communication/outreach options (see list in Chapter 7) and create an appropriate outreach/ communication plan and schedule accordingly.

Based on where you are in your career, spend time considering/evaluating all possible options, asking yourself the following:

What is the appropriate "mix" of marketing, client development and/or client service tools I should plan for and execute for each of my primary targets/markets that will result in appropriate, regular contact and new/additional work from the targets/markets I have defined above?

APPENDIX 2

STRATEGIC CONTACT ANALYSIS CHECKLIST

GROWTH STARTS AND STOPS WITH EACH CONTACT YOU
ALREADY HAVE
GOAL = MAKE THE MOST OF EACH CONTACT/RELATIONSHIP

**QUESTIONS TO ASK YOURSELF ABOUT EACH OF YOUR
(BEST FIRST), INDIVIDUAL CLIENTS/REFERRAL SOURCES:**

1. On a scale of 1-10, with 10 being OUTSTANDING, what is the overall strength of this relationship?

2. Do I want to/need to enhance/improve this relationship? If so, how precisely?

3. Should I/can I add value to this relationship? Can I make it more mutually reciprocal? I.e. more of a "win-win"? If so, how precisely?

4. Am I CERTAIN or am I ASSUMING this client is 100% satisfied with our services? And I am doing everything possible to provide exceptional service? If not, what else can I/we do? I.e. send a client satisfaction survey or discuss it?

5. What other problems, either developing, future and/or latent might this client have or be facing? Am I 100% sure they know our firm's capability to service them in these areas? If so, what

other areas could we provide service? Whom do we need to know/meet with? Can we/I ask for a referral to that person(s)?

6. Are there other subsidiaries or divisions of this company where we could be doing work? If so, what? Whom do we need to know/meet with? Can we/I ask for a referral to the appropriate people/decision-makers?

7. Whom does this client/contact know that uses outside law firms like ours? I.e. other General Counsel in companies I would like to be doing work for. If so, what company and who in that company? Can we/I ask for a referral?

8. What else can I/we possibly do to enhance, improve, augment and/or further develop this relationship?

9. Other:

APPENDIX 3

KEY CLIENT CHECKLIST

Important Questions to Ask Self re: Each "Key" Client and/or Key Referral Source

Have I and/or the Main Relationship Partner?......

- ❖ Been in touch with this client in last month – especially if there is no open/active case/matter?
- ❖ Personally visited this client at their place of business (off the current matter and non-billable) just to see how things were going with the business?
- ❖ Voluntarily devoted non-billable time to attending this client's management and/or annual meetings?
- ❖ Attended any industry event (meeting, trade show or conference) with them/for them? Or initiated a discussion/invitation to do so?
- ❖ Specifically invited this client to attend and participate in a practice, industry, or client team meeting in order to brief our team/group on new developments in their company or their industry?
- ❖ Introduced this client to a person of potential/strategic importance to them, a person that could be a potential future

customer and/or someone else they could benefit from knowing?

❖ Provided periodic, non-billable check in/status updates even when there is nothing active on their cases/matters and/or do not have anything open/pending for them?

❖ Proactively interviewed them and subsequently drafted and circulated a written report on what each client representative told you about their and their company's specific needs, issues, developments, trends? Have you obtained a copy of and personally read the strategic plan of each key client's company?

❖ Ascertained if there are internal efforts to subscribe to, read, and circulate pertinent clippings from this client's news feed, trade publications, cases filed and other sources? If not, should I initiate the discussion?

❖ Discussed and established a direct technology link as relevant and appropriate? And/or if one is in place, review its performance with them to consider updates/upgrades?

❖ Developed written service standards/plans, which identifies how I/our team are working to address this client's needs and stay abreast of issues, trends? And scheduled accordingly?

❖ Created a relationship map, who knows whom, who know what including main and back-up contacts and communicated it to them?

❖ Do we have a coordinated and automated system/method and tools to stay-in-touch as appropriate with each key client representative as appropriate?

❖ Are we connected on LinkedIn to all key client representatives?

❖ Do we/does our firm "follow" the client on LinkedIn and Twitter?

❖ Have regularly scheduled (as appropriate), internal Key Client Team meetings to maintain and upgrade the above?

APPENDIX 4

PROFESSIONALS QUOTED OR CITED

Catherine MacDonagh Alman,
www.linkedin.com/in/catherinemacdonagh
Richard Amador, www.linkedin.com/in/richardamador/
Robert Ambrogi, www.linkedin.com/in/robertambrogi/
Jason Barnwell, www.linkedin.com/in/jbarnwell/
Lucy Endel Bassli, www.linkedin.com/in/lucybassli/
Ralph Baxter, www.linkedin.com/in/ralph-baxter-20b00092/
Keith Block, www.linkedin.com/in/keith-block-516a1811/
Connie Brenton, www.linkedin.com/in/conniebrenton/
Toby Brown, www.linkedin.com/in/tobinbrown/
Liam Brown, www.linkedin.com/in/liamjmbrown/
Craig Budner, www.linkedin.com/in/craig-budner-02bbb0b/
Lavinia Calvert, www.linkedin.com/in/calla444/
Jeff Carr, www.linkedin.com/in/jeff-carr-651967a5/
Thomas Choberka, www.linkedin.com/in/thomaschoberka/
Clayton Christensen, www.linkedin.com/in/claytonchristensen/
Pamela Cone, www.linkedin.com/in/pamelacone/
Bill Conerly, www.linkedin.com/in/businomics/
Michelle Browning Coughlin, www.linkedin.com/in/michelle-browning-coughlin-18b5a019/

Stephen Covey, www.linkedin.com/in/stephen-m-r-covey-6400191a5/

John Croft, www.linkedin.com/in/johnpkcroft/

Stephen Crossman, www.linkedin.com/in/stephen-crossman-65b6859/

David Cunningham, www.linkedin.com/in/davidbcunningham/

Brian Duffy, www.linkedin.com/in/brianlduffy/

Susan Saltonstall Duncan, www.linkedin.com/in/susan-saltonstall-duncan-34164011/

Justin Essner, www.linkedin.com/in/justinessner/

Deborah Brightman Farone, www.linkedin.com/in/deborahfarone/

Ross Fishman, www.linkedin.com/in/rossfishman/

Susan Freeman, www.linkedin.com/in/susancfreeman/

Ron Freidmann, www.linkedin.com/in/ronfriedmann/

Walter Frick, www.linkedin.com/in/walter-frick-412b9512/

Robert Glazer, www.linkedin.com/in/glazer/

James Goodnow, www.linkedin.com/in/jamesgoodnow/

Carol Schiro, Greenwald, www.linkedin.com/in/carolschirogreenwald/

Susan Hackett, www.linkedin.com/in/susanhackett/

Jay Harrington, www.linkedin.com/in/jayharrington/

Tom Holland, www.linkedin.com/in/tom-holland-25976086/

Mary Jennings, www.linkedin.com/in/mary-jennings-clm-sphr-shrm-scp-1a787612/

Sharon Jones, www.linkedin.com/in/sharonejones/

Brad Karp, www.linkedin.com/in/brad-karp-25021a2a/

Jeff Katzin, www.linkedin.com/in/jeffkatzin/

David Kesmodel, www.linkedin.com/in/david-kesmodel-653a19/

Nancy Koehn, www.linkedin.com/in/jeff-carr-651967a5/

Rick Kushel, www.linkedin.com/in/rickkushel/

Susan Rairdon Lambreth, www.linkedin.com/in/susan-raridon-lambreth-b48971a/

Colin Levy, www.linkedin.com/in/cslcorporatecounsel/

Adrian Lurssen, www.linkedin.com/in/lurssen/

Olga Mack, www.linkedin.com/in/olgamack/

David Maister (retired), davidmaister.com/

Kim Easterle Mattes, www.linkedin.com/in/kimmattes/

Michael McGee, www.linkedin.com/in/michaelmcgee2/

Patrick McKenna, www.linkedin.com/in/patrickjmckenna/

Saul McLeod, www.linkedin.com/in/saulmcleod/

Deborah McMurray, www.linkedin.com/in/deborahmcmurray/

Caitlin "Cat" Moon, www.linkedin.com/in/caitlinmoon/

Jason Morris, https://www.linkedin.com/in/jason-morris-09684023/

Jeff Morris, www.linkedin.com/in/jeffmorrismediation/

Mark Murphy, www.linkedin.com/in/markamurphy/

Steve Nelson, www.linkedin.com/in/steve-nelson-40b48b2/

Jack Newton, www.linkedin.com/in/jackbnewton/

Jason Noble, www.linkedin.com/in/janoble/

Martin O'Flynn, www.linkedin.com/in/systemicmind/

Maddy Osman, www.linkedin.com/in/madelineosman/

Howard "Bud" Phillips, www.linkedin.com/in/howardbudphillips/

Victor Prince, www.linkedin.com/in/victorprince/

Michael Raynor, www.linkedin.com/in/meraynor/

Jeff Reade, www.linkedin.com/in/jeffreade/

John Reikes, www.linkedin.com/in/john-reikes-b983ab5/

Kimberly Rice, www.linkedin.com/in/kimberlyalfordrice/

Larry Richard, www.linkedin.com/in/lawyerbrain

Gerry Riskin, www.linkedin.com/in/gerryriskin/

Gina Rubel, www.linkedin.com/in/ginafuriarubel/

Audrey Rubin, www.linkedin.com/in/audreyrubin/

Kathryn Rubino, www.linkedin.com/in/kathryn-rubino-6ba7854/

Michael Rynowecer, www.linkedin.com/in/michael-rynowecer-0488304/

Kirk Sanderson, www.linkedin.com/in/kirksanderson/

Julie Savarino, www.linkedin.com/in/juliesavarino/

Sally Schmidt, www.linkedin.com/in/sallyjschmidt/

Eric Seeger, www.linkedin.com/in/eseeger/

Roy Sexton, www.linkedin.com/in/roysexton

John Sharkey, www.linkedin.com/in/johnsharkey2/

Caren Ulrich Stacy, www.linkedin.com/in/caren-ulrich-stacy-5019691/

Howard, Stevenson, www.linkedin.com/in/howard-stevenson-b460221/

Dan Tacone, www.linkedin.com/in/dantacone/

Cammie Teems, www.bestwaycorp.us/

Gabriel Teninbaum, www.linkedin.com/in/gabriel-teninbaum-6a34676/

Jia Wertz, www.linkedin.com/in/jiawertz/

Nick Wignall, www.linkedin.com/in/nick-wignall-20880816a/

Kurtis Wilder, www.linkedin.com/in/kurtis-wilder-51962a184/

ENDNOTES

[1] "Forgetting Curve." *www.Wikipedia.org*. 20 Apr 2020.

[2] Ralph Baxter (www.RalphBaxter.com) served as Chairman and CEO of Orrick for over twenty-five years. He successfully led and steered Orrick through several economic recessions and upheavals. Ralph is one of the world's leading, most respected, admired, and emulated managing partners in law firm history.

[3] Savarino, Julie. "Six Best Practices in Client Relations for the New Normal." *LinkedIn.com*. 16 Apr 2020.

[4] Robert Glazer (www.RobertGlazer.com), Founder and CEO of Acceleration Partners. (www.Acceleration Partners.com)

[5] Savarino, Julie. "What Law Firm Clients Want and Need Now." *LinkedIn.com*. March 2020.

[6] This post was adapted from these two LinkedIn posts:, one by Caitlin Moon, "In-house lawyers to big law: enough already" and one by Julie Savarino: www.linkedin.com/posts/caitlinmoon_in-house-lawyers-to-big-law-enough-already-activity-6648941409200074752-aY2P; and www.linkedin.com/posts/juliesavarino_generalcounsel-lawfirms-legalweek2020-activity-6630635063698563072-5Lx3.

[7] Osman, Maddy. "Mind-blowing LinkedIn Statistics and Facts." 10 Apr 2020. *www.kinsta.com*.

[8] Robino, Kathryn. "Paul Weiss's Bold Leadership on Coronavirus Pro Bono Efforts." *Above the Law*. 17 May 2020.

[9] "William Bernbach." https://en.wikipedia.org/wiki/William_Bernbach.

[10] Gerry Riskin (www.GerryRiskin.com) is one the world's leading advisors and consultants for law and other professional services firms. Over thirty-five years, he has worked with many firms to help

them successfully weather several economic downturns. Gerry is the Founder of Edge International_(www.Edge.ai).

[11] Kesmodel, David. "We've Been Here Before." *Wall Street Journal,* 23 Apr 2009.

[12] Holland, Tom and Katzin, Jeff. "Beyond the Downturn: Recession Strategies to Take the Lead." *www.Bain.com.* 16 May 2019.

[13] Conerly, Bill. "4 Lessons on Recession Business Preparation." *Forbes.com.* 6 June 2019.

[14] SunTrust. "The Move to Divest." *www.SunTrust.com/resource-center.*

[15] SunTrust. "Managing your Business in the next Downturn." *Atlanta Business Chronicle.* 4 Dec 2019.

[16] Frick, Walter. "How to Survive a Recession and Thrive Afterward." *Harvard Business Review.* May-June 2019.

[17] Altman Weil. "Law Firms in Transition 2013: An Altman Weil Flash Survey." *www.AltmanWeil.com.*

[18] Ambrogi, Robert. "New Law Firm LOP Partnership Aims to Cut Corporate Legal Spend by Half." *Above the Law.* 30 April 2018.

[19] Association of Corporate Council. *Value Challenge.* www.acc.com/services-inititiatives/value-challenge.

[20] McLeod, Saul. "Maslow's Hierarchy of Needs." *SimplyPsychology.com.* 20 Mar 2020.

[21] Gregory, Christina. "The Five Stages of Grief." www.psycom.net. 2020.

[22] "Richard Branson." https://en.wikipedia.org/wiki/Richard_Branson

[23] *How People Learn: Brain, Mind, Experience, and School,* Chapter 8. The National Academies Press. www.nap.edu.

[24] Larson, Erik. "New Research: Diversity Inclusion Leads to Better Decision-Making at Work." *Forbes.* 21 Sept 2017.

[25] "Peter Salovey." *www.wikipedia.org.*

[26] Wignall, Nick. "Personal Growth: 4 Things Emotionally Intelligent People Don't Do." *Medium.* 4 Apr 2020.

[27] The Myers & Briggs Foundation. *Myersbriggs.org.* 2020.

[28] Richard, Larry. "Herding Cats: The Lawyer Personality Revealed." *ManagingPartnerForum.org.*

[29] "DISC Assessment." *www.wikipedia.org.*

[30] "Who Do I Want to Be During COVID-19." *www.colorado.edu/hr.* 9 Apr 2020.

[31] "Unleash Potential: Conscious and Unconscious Bias." *www.vanderbilt.edu/diversity.*

[32] Miller, Alex P. "Want Less Biased Decisions? Use Algorithms." *Harvard Business Journal. 26* July2018.

[33] Christiansen, Clayton M., Raynor, Michael E., McDonald. "What is Disruptive Innovation." *Harvard Business Review.* Dec 2015.

[34] Adapted from "The Evolution to Modern Legal (143)." Jason Barnwell. *www.LegalEvolution.org.* 29 March 2020.

[35] Schmidt, Sally J. "Earning a Client's Trust." *www.attorneyatwork.com.* 19 Mar 2020.

[36] Winfrey, Graham. "3 Life Lessons Tom Hanks Learned from Playing the Kindest Man, Mr. Rogers." *www.inc.com.* 7 Feb 2020.

[37] Cherry, Kendra. "The Psychology of Forgetting and Why Memory Fails." *www.verywellmind.com.* 7 Feb 2020.

[38] ContentPilot. "How Do They Measure Up? 2020 AmLaw Global 50 Websites." *www.contentpilot.com.* 1 Sept 2019.

[39] "75 Customer Service Facts, Quotes, & Statistics." *www.helpscout.com.*

[40] JD Supra Perspectives. "Taking Law Firm Business Development to the Next Level." *www.jdsupra.com.* 11 July 2019.

[41] Ironpaper. "What is a Qualified Lead? How to Set Criteria." *www.ironpaper.com.* 29 Jan 2019.

[42] Bort, Julie. "Jeff Bezos Asks Himself this Simple Question When Planning for the Future." *Business Insider.* 6 June 2019.

[43] "Well Actually, Americans say customer service is better than ever." *https://about.AmericanExpress.com.* 15 Dec 2019.

[44] Lambreth, Susan Raridon. "Why Your Business Professional Team is Critical to Your Firm's Viability Right Now." *www.legalexecutiveinstitute.com*. 27 Apr 2020.

[45] Baxter, Ralph. "A Time to Learn Three Questions Law Firms Should Ask to Prepare for the 'New Normal.'" *www.legalservicestoday.com*. 5 May 2020.

[46] LePan, Nicholas. "Visualizing the History of Pandemics" *www.visualcapitalist.com*. 14 Mar 2020.

[47] Ramalingam, B. "Tools for Knowledge and Learning, ODI Toolkit." London: ODI. 2006.

[48] Catherine Alman MacDonagh is the founder of the Legal Lean Sigma Institute (http://legalleansigma.com).

[49] McKenna, Patrick J., Rynowecer, Michael B. "Having a Real Industry Focus: Clients Value Firms that Have a 'Deep' Industry Focus — So, Do You? (Part 2)" *www.legalexecutiveinstitute.com*. 10 Mar 2020.

[50] Mack, Olga. "Notes to My Legal Self." *www.linkedin.com*. April 2020.

[51] Friedmann, Ron. "Rethinking How Lawyers Work Post-Crisis." *www.prismlegal.com*. April 2020.

[52] Gabriel Teninbaum is currently writing a book on Productizing the Law (exact title TBD), due out in late-2020.

[53] Levy, Colin. "Some thoughts on legal technology and legal innovation." *www.LinkedIn.com*. April 2020.

[54] Wertz, Jia. "Don't Spend 5 Times More Attracting New Customers. Nurture the Existing Ones." *www.Forbes.com*. 12 Sep 2018.

[55] Fishman, Ross. "Cross-selling Sucks. Here are 18 Reasons Why (Part 2)." *www.fishmanmarketing.com*. 13 Oct 2015.

[56] McKenna, Patrick J., Rynowecer, Michael B. "Having a Real Industry Focus: Clients Value Firms that have a Deep Industry Focus, Pt. 2." *www.legalexecutiveinstitute.com*. 10 Mar 2020.

[57] Intapp. "Intapp Debuts Oneplace for Marketing." *www.intapp.com*. 31 Mar 2020.

[58] Duncan, Susan Saltonstall. "How to Enable Value with Clients: Part 2." *www.linkedin.com*. 15 Apr 2020.

[59] Blount, Sally and Leinwand, Paul. "Why Are we Here?" *Harvard Business Review.* Nov-Dec 2019.1

[60] Elevate. "Equitability and Inclusion Report." *https://elevateservices.com*. 2019.

[61] Since almost all professional services firms are privately-held entities, for most there is no legal requirement to publicly report D&I information (except for law firms in England and Wales in which are required, by the U.K government to compile and report comprehensive diversity statistics about their entire workforce, including practicing lawyers *and* all other employees every two years).

[62] Gaudiano, Paulo. "Here is Why Diversity and Inclusion are Disconnected and How to Fix That." *www.forbes.com*. 4 May 2020.

[63] Nelson, Steve. "As Competition Changes, Law Firms Increasingly Look to Big 4 for CMOs." *www.linkedin.com*. 31 Mar 2020.

[64] "GreenbergTraurig Announces the Founding of Recurve." *www.gtlaw.com*. 11 June 2019.

[65] Murphy, Mark. "Neuroscience Explains Why You Need to Write Down Your Goals, If You Actually Want to Achieve Them." *www.forbes.com*. 15 Apr 2018.

[66] Sandberg, Jerry. "Rise of False Deadline Means Truly Urgent Often Gets Done Late." *Wall Street Journal.* 23 Jan 2007.

[67] Murphy, Mark. "Neuroscience Explains Why You Need to Write You're your Goals if you Actually Want to Achieve Something." *Forbes.* 15 Apr 2018.

Made in the USA
Monee, IL
13 November 2021